MORE THAN PETTICOATS

Remarkable New Hampshire Women

Gail Underwood Parker

gpp®

Guilford, Connecticut

To my father, James Horton Underwood (1919–2008). His lifetime of letters and stories as Father Jacob and Jay Han Won surrounded us with the magic of words. His encouraged us to believe that any dream is a possibility that we could attempt, and his confidence in our potential was unwavering. He never tired of hearing my excited discoveries of some fascinating tidbit about one of these women. He delighted in simply sitting in the room while I typed, supporting me with his presence as he read or worked a crossword puzzle. Despite his failing health he always insisted I make the time, even if only fifteen minutes a day, to continue my writing, to work toward my dreams. Thank you, Daddy.

To buy books in quantity for corporate use
or incentives, call **(800) 962-0973**
or e-mail **premiums@GlobePequot.com**.

Text design by Nancy Freeborn
Map by Daniel Lloyd © Morris Book Publishing LLC

Library of Congress Cataloging-in-Publication Data
Parker, Gail Underwood.
   More than petticoats : remarkable New Hampshire women / Gail Underwood Parker.
      p. cm.
   ISBN 978-0-7627-4002-4
   1. Women—New Hampshire—Biography. 2. Women—New Hampshire—History. 3. New Hampshire—Biography. I. Title.
   CT3262.N4P37 2009
   920.7209742—dc22

2008050404

Contents

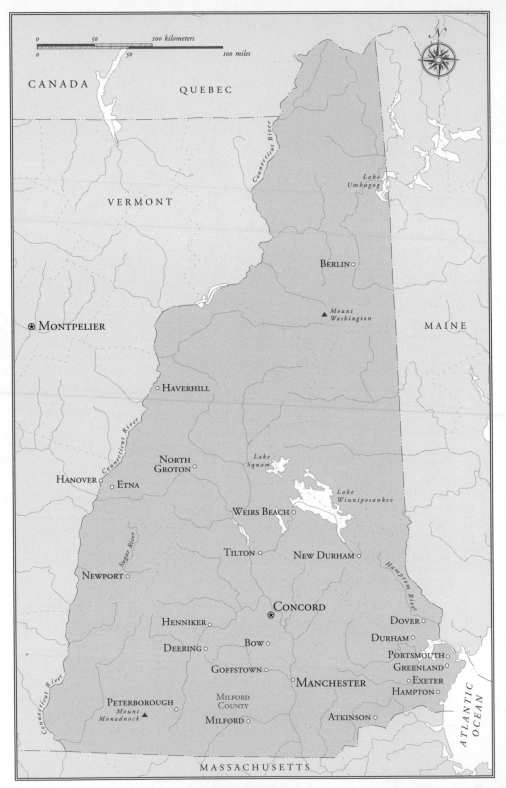

New hampshire

ACKNOWLEDGMENTS

For their help in researching details about the wonderful women in this book I am deeply indebted to my New Hampshire resources: Paul Hughes and Greenland's Lane Memorial Library; Betty Moore and the Tuck Museum in Hampton; Roland Goodbody and the staff at Milne Collections, University of New Hampshire; Bill Copely and the New Hampshire Historical Society; Stephanie Sullivan and the Perkins Institute for the Blind; Evelyn Gerson; Valerie Cunningham; the Harriet Wilson Project; and the library staffs of Newburyport, New Durham, Hampton, Lane Memorial, Berlin, Concord, and Portsmouth. Thanks also to Donald Sloane, Donald Bisson, the people of Berlin, Ken Leidner, New Hampshire Veterans Association, and the families of Lotte Jacobi and Hilda Brungot, particularly Catherine and George.

At home in Maine I am grateful to Don, Cathy, and Ann at the Portland Public Library for constant encouragement during many marathon microfilm sessions, and the staff of Cape Elizabeth's Thomas Memorial Library who dealt with stack after stack of books and articles ordered through interlibrary loan.

Without Hayden Atwood's help my struggles with the world of commas would be common-knowledge. He has been an indispensable, cheerful, and expert proofreader. I would not have been able to find time to make all the needed research trips to New Hampshire without Jennifer Alward's child care help. Destry Oldham-

Sibley's calm support helped me stay sane amidst ever-changing chaos. I thank Pat Miller for understanding the priority this project took. A unique appreciation goes to Ted and the gang at Ocean House Pizza who allowed the back booth to be my pseudo writing office, spreading notes, outlines, and computer around pizza, pesto, and ice-cold soda, always stopping to ask what chapter I was working on, cheer me on, and send me back to work.

My family is the steel framework of support for all I do. My brother John and sister Laurel; my daughters Alexis, Anna, Miriam, Leah, and Belinda; my special kiddos Mariah, Eric, Shawn, and Sasha; and my Boston grandchildren Jacob, Ezra, Nora, Lena, and Nathan. They have all understood when work on the book affected family times—and still encouraged me. Thanks also to Julie Marsh, GPP project manager, for shepherding this manuscript through its final checks and changes. And a heartfelt thank you to my editor, Megan Hiller, for giving me the chance to discover these marvelous women and inhabit their lives. Gratitude also for her exceptional patience and Globe Pequot's understanding as life seemed determined to interfere with the writing of this book.

INTRODUCTION

Living in Maine for almost forty years I was comfortable researching and writing *It Happened in Maine,* but starting *More Than Petticoats: Remarkable New Hampshire Women* was like striking up a conversation with a long-ignored neighbor. New England neighbors often go their own ways, cordial from a distance, yet independent and separate. But sometimes a moment happens while shoveling parallel driveways after a winter storm or while waiting for a school bus with the children. Someone goes beyond the courteous nod or weather comment, and points in common are discovered. Soon the neighbor is an interesting person, not just a name on the mailbox. Many of the richest friendships begin with unexpected intersections.

Researching this book I began tentatively reaching out to my down-the-way "neighbor" state and now am richer for the women I have met. I found Ona Judge who fled the most powerful, admired man in America, and found safety and freedom in New Hampshire. Like me, Sarah Hale was a single parent and working mom. She inspired me with her accomplishments: a permanent piece of childhood, a lasting tribute to America's fight for independence, and a national holiday, all while maintaining a professional life admirable even by today's standards. Laura Bridgman, although often overlooked, was a template for Helen Keller and all who followed. I love the nerve and determination of Marilla Ricker, attempting to run for governor before women could even vote. Marian MacDowell initially sacrificed her career for that of her famous husband but later far eclipsed his place in the artistic world through her own vision and action. One discovery after another led me to the thirteen women whose stories I am honored to share with readers.

These thirteen women are a mosaic. White and black, Jewish and Scandinavian, rich and poor, convicted and lawyer, prodigy and late bloomer, respected and scorned, adamantly religious and anti-religion, immigrants and descendants of colonists. They are all worth meeting. Their stories should be known and told. While reading these pages, I suspect you will discover unexpected common bonds with these women. I am sure you will be captivated by their stories.

There are so many more friends to discover, lives to explore. The guideline for this series is women born before 1900, eliminating Elizabeth Yates and many recent outstanding women. Women like Celia Thaxter I left out because their lives are already well-documented. Others, such as Dinah Whipple and her school, lacked enough detail to share. There are many more fascinating stories to be told, common bonds to uncover. So, if these women's stories inspire you, go down the road to a library, or go to a senior member of your community. Start a conversation. You may discover someone wonderful with a story that must be told.

EUNICE "GOODY" COLE

ca. 1590–1680

Falsely Accused

EUNICE COLE SAT IN THE PRISONER'S DOCK of New Hampshire's county court of Norfolk listening to the litany of accusations. Neighbor after neighbor stepped forward to make their awful claims about Goodwife "Goody" Eunice Cole.

Town selectmen stood and claimed she had caused the death of a cow and a sheep in spiteful retaliation for the town's refusal to give her charity wood for the winter. Neighbor Thomas Philbrick recounted a fierce argument, testifying that Cole had threatened that if any of his calves came on her land and ate her grass, she hoped it would poison them or they would choke on it. Philbrick said he soon discovered two cows missing. One was never found, and though the second turned up later, it immediately fell sick and died within a week. Abraham Drake, another neighbor, testified that after he returned a cow the Coles had lost, an ungrateful Goody Cole blamed him for the cow's death a week later. She threatened revenge on Drake's cattle. When three of his cattle were lost that summer, Drake immediately blamed Eunice's curse.

This doll was one of those sold in 1938 at the Hampton Beach ceremonies to rehabilitate Eunice "Goody" Cole's reputation. The urn contains ashes of the trial documents burned that day. The urn and doll are on display at the Tuck Museum in Hampton, New Hampshire.

Next came some of the women who had so often gossiped about Eunice. Goodwife Sobriety Moulton and Goodwife Sleeper swore they had been talking about Goody Cole when they suddenly heard the sounds of scraping against the window frame. Frightened, they checked outside but found nothing near the window to explain the noise. Returning inside and resuming their conversation, they said the sound returned even louder. Each time the women checked outside they found nothing, but each time they resumed their gossip the unexplained noises returned, louder and more frightening.

Goody Marston and Susanna Palmer testified that they, too, had seen evidence of Goody Cole's witchcraft.

Even children came forward to accuse Eunice. They claimed Goody Cole was in league with the Evil One and was even bold enough to chastise him. They described peeking in Goody Cole's window and seeing a small black dwarf with a red cap sitting at her table. They watched as he would get riled up and be brought back under control by Goody Cole cuffing his ears. Others stepped forward, charging that this alliance between Goodwife Cole and the Devil was the source of her power to frighten, injure, curse, and punish anyone who offended her.

One after another, throughout the long day of September 4, the people of Hampton testified against the old woman glaring at them from the dock. Edward Rawson, the court's secretary, dutifully recorded each claim of threat, each curse, and each supposed act of collusion with the Devil. They even recorded official depositions about times that Goody Cole called someone's mother a whore. The procession of witnesses begged the court to pronounce Goody Cole a witch and sentence her immediately. When all had finished, it was time for Eunice to await the verdict.

The 1656 trial for witchcraft was hardly Eunice's first brush with the law in colonial New Hampshire. Her husband William Cole had first come to Watertown, colonial Massachusetts, as a servant, and then followed John Wheelwright to Exeter, New Hampshire. He lived in Exeter and eventually obtained a grant of land in the new wilderness settlement that would become Hampton. The April 30, 1640, grant confirmed "5 acres for a house lot as gr. And 2 of Salt Marsh where it may be found, 45 acres of planting ground, adjoining to his house lott." Eunice and William built their new home in 1644 on a small rise overlooking the Hampton River and adjacent marshes. The Coles also held one of 147 shares of common lands in Hampton. They made the move from Exeter in 1645; William and Eunice had seats assigned in the meetinghouse; and early town records show William drew share #38 in the common ox grazing area in 1651. But soon those same records give hints that the Coles were not getting along with the community. The tax list for 1653 showed the Coles were the very last of Hampton's seventy-two households to pay their taxes. A series of petty disagreements put the Coles in and out of court on charges of slander, illegal withholding of pigs, and other misdemeanors.

By all accounts Goody Cole was an obnoxious, spiteful old woman. When she needed help in the winter, rather than ask politely, Eunice demanded that town selectmen give her free wood. Known for cursing and threatening those who opposed her, Eunice Cole was almost universally despised. Apparently not an attractive woman to begin with, Goody Cole cared little about her physical appearance, making her the target of taunts by the town children, who often played tricks on her. The journals of early Hampton historian Edmund Willoughby Toppan describe Eunice Cole as "a fruitful source of vexation to the good people of Hampton for a long series of years."

In seventeenth-century New England, belief in the Devil as an active power was common, and superstitions abounded. Many houses routinely displayed a horseshoe nail over the front door to ward off witches. People who were quarrelsome or who broke the moral or social codes of the community were often accused of witchcraft, and women were targeted more than four times as often as men, particularly childless women over the age of forty. Eunice Cole was an almost natural target because of her circumstances, her behavior, and her abrasive personality. Now she stood accused with no one but her husband William to defend her.

The court found Eunice guilty of practicing witchcraft and sentenced her to be flogged, then imprisoned for the remainder of her life or until released by the court. The flogging was carried out immediately, but the colonial territory of New Hampshire had no facilities for life imprisonment. The town made arrangements for Goody to be incarcerated in Boston. In those days, the cost of imprisonment was born by the convicted or the prisoner's family. The cost was eight pounds a year (roughly forty dollars). Eunice was transported to Boston and jailed. William paid the cost first by depleting their meager savings and then by selling off pieces of his land. On November 3, 1659, William petitioned the General Court for relief. Nearly eighty years old, he was frail, unable to work, and "near perishing." In exchange for the town's taking responsibility for the care of both Coles for the remainder of their lives, William allowed the town of Hampton to take over the rest of the Cole estate, leaving him only a small house in which to live. The town sent money to Boston to pay the cost of Eunice's imprisonment until the value of the estate was totally spent, but then stopped sending payment.

Still in the Boston prison, Goody Cole petitioned the court to be released to return to Hampton and care for William, who was in poor health. The court said they would release her on two conditions: she pay the amount of her past due board, and she leave the court's jurisdiction within a month. With no money or resources to pay the overdue costs, Eunice remained in custody. William died May 26, 1661. Five days earlier he had made a will leaving Eunice a few clothes and personal items she had left with him when sent to jail. William left the house to a Thomas Webster in gratitude for helping care for him in his last years.

With no money from Eunice, and the town of Hampton failing to pay her board, the bill climbed. When eight years passed with no payment, the colonial court took action. At that time, public officials could be jailed for nonpayment of civic debts, so the court signed a warrant to arrest Hampton's selectmen for lack of payment. Boston jailor William Salter went to Hampton and, on July 14, 1664, selectman Thomas Marston was arrested pending payment of the balance due. The town scrambled and came up with the amount due using the proceeds of small fines levied by the town. The next year town records show that John Coffin delivered a sum of eight pounds to William Salter for the continued maintenance of prisoner Eunice Cole.

In 1665 Eunice again petitioned the court for her freedom. This time the court's only requirement was that she relocate outside the Norfolk court's jurisdiction. By this time Eunice was too old and feeble to support herself, much less find a new home. She remained in jail and Hampton continued to pay.

After almost fifteen years in jail Eunice was finally released and returned to Hampton. With no husband, no home, and no friends, Eunice was dependent on the charity of the town that had apparently decided it was cheaper to keep her there than pay her jail board. In 1671 the town selectmen ordered the townsfolk to take turns supporting Eunice one week at a time "in the order in which they dwelt." Eunice was given the use of an old shack near the Meeting House Green at Rand's Hill. Turn by turn, each family provided her food and cut her firewood as needed.

Apparently Eunice's years in prison had done nothing to improve her disposition or her demeanor. The new arrangement lasted barely a year before the gossip again spread accusations of witchery, curses, and odd behavior. In October 1671 Eunice was again arraigned on charges of witchcraft. This time there were new claims. Now people stepped forward to claim Eunice had appeared in the guise of a dog, an eagle, and a cat, changing shapes to meet the Devil's needs. Others charged that she had "enticed" a young girl named Ann Smith to live with her. They claimed she had lured the nine-year-old into an orchard with promises of plums and a baby. Ann claimed that when she refused, Eunice hit her with a stone, changed into a dog, ran up a tree, then changed into an eagle and flew away. Once more Eunice was charged with witchcraft and in April 1673 the Salisbury Court ordered Eunice to Boston to await trial. She was over eighty years old.

The presiding magistrate, Major Richard Waldron, found that there was suspicion of her being a witch and that "upon examination of the testimony, the Court vehemently suspects her so to be." Pending proof during trial he ordered Eunice be imprisoned "with a lock to be kept on her leg" until the trial was complete and verdict read. Once again the town selectmen of Hampton, Province of New Hampshire, were ordered to pay the costs of Eunice's confinement.

Perhaps the Boston courts remembered what a problem Eunice had been the last time she was convicted and jailed in Boston. Perhaps they had sympathy for the old woman, despite the charges. Clearly the court found grounds to believe Eunice consorted with the Devil. Yet Major Waldron handed down a verdict with most unusual wording: "In ye case of Unis Cole now prisoner att ye Bar not Legally guilty according to Inditement butt just ground of vehement suspissyon of her having had familyarryty with the devil."

Eunice returned to Hampton, New Hampshire, and lived out her few remaining years in abject poverty. She was given a small hut near present-day Hampton Academy and, once again, townspeople furnished her food. Bitter and isolated, Eunice was hated and persecuted by the citizens who never stopped fearing and scorning her. When she died, there was no reference in the town records of her burial, no marker for her grave, nothing but rumors of superstitious mistreatment of her body and grave site.

Over the following twenty years, Eunice Cole's place in the folklore of witchcraft trials was completely overshadowed by the hysteria that swept through Salem, Massachusetts. But her story didn't end, buried beneath the flashier trials in Salem. Fast-forward more than two hundred and fifty years. The colonies have become the United States, the province has become the state of New Hampshire, and the edge-of-wilderness hamlet of Hampton is a bustling New England village.

The most unexpected change in 1938 in Hampton was a recently formed organization that was gaining national attention. A small group of townspeople, led by a colorful newspaperman named Bill Cram, banded together to form "The Society in Hampton Beach for the Apprehension of Those Falsely Accusing Eunice 'Goody' Cole of Having Familiarity with the Devil." At the start, the society had more words in its name than members, but it had a cause. The stated goal was to rehabilitate Eunice Cole's reputation and standing in the community. The group grew and the story spread. These modern citizens of Hampton regretted the fact that its early citizens had falsely accused Goody Cole and had persecuted her for so many years. The society stated its determination to remove that stain from its town's history by official action.

At the March 8, 1938, town meeting, the society's carefully crafted and sponsored Article 16 was read. Letters urging its passage were also read, including one from Haverhill, Massachusetts, resident Arnold Philbrick. He was a direct descendent of the Thomas Philbrick whose testimony helped convict Eunice at the first trial. His only request was that those who testified against her not be vilified for their misguided actions. Residents spoke in support of the resolution and then it was moved, seconded, and quickly passed. Local newspapers covered the story.

The unusual story quickly found its way into the national media. Some gave passing notice to the planned events, others expanded the coverage to look at the history of witchcraft and superstition past and present. Often the coverage included bits of folklore mixed in as facts. Some reported sightings of Goody Cole's ghost on dark nights. A full-page, illustrated article in Missouri's *St. Louis Dispatch* bore the headline "Buried With a Stake Through Her Heart" and included grave site desecrations among the injustices for which the town of Hampton was trying to make amends. Many magazine articles included references to John Greenleaf Whittier's poem *The Wreck at Rivermouth*. The poem details the story of a ship and passengers lost at sea, having been cursed by an angry Goody Cole after a verbal spat with the crew. Few pointed out that the shipwreck in question took place after Eunice was already incarcerated in Boston, making any verbal altercation with the sailors in Hampton impossible. The poetic license made for better narrative poetry than journalistic fact.

Radio joined in as well. The town meeting was reenacted for NBC Radio coast to coast. Commentators used the occasion to assess the status of superstition in current society and to celebrate the progress made since the paranoid chaos of the early witch hysterias. The publicity continued as plans were made for the special ceremony to carry out the town's mandate to exonerate Eunice.

Finally the grand day arrived. The boulevard along Hampton Beach was closed and the street was filled with folding chairs for the crowds later reported numbering three thousand. Ceremonies began promptly at 2:00 p.m., with the Hampton Beach Concert Band playing a march composed especially for the occasion, followed by an invocation by the pastor of the oldest parish in New

Hampshire. There were musical selections, official greetings from the governor, and addresses from participants ranging from town officials to the widow of famed magician Harry Houdini, who had flown from California especially for the memorial.

Under the striped canopy town selectmen offered certified copies of original documents from Eunice Cole's trial. They were ceremoniously burned and mixed with dirt from near Goody's well and from her "last reputed resting place." "The Society in Hampton Beach for the Apprehension of Those Falsely Accusing Eunice 'Goody' Cole of Having Familiarity with the Devil" had finally succeeded. By town vote and civic action, the accusations against Eunice Cole were declared false, her innocence of the charges given official status.

Visitors to modern-day New Hampshire can still find reminders of Eunice Cole. The ashes of the burned documents are still in the Hampton Historical Society's Tuck Museum, but not in the fancy urn pictured in news articles of 1938. A simple metal canister engraved with Eunice's name and the dates of her conviction and "exoneration" is so darkened by time that the letters are nearly illegible. The canister is displayed in a glass case with one of the Goody Cole dolls made for the celebration. The full-page article from the *St. Louis Dispatch* hangs under glass on the adjoining wall. A large boulder set upright on the museum grounds stands in for the unknown burial site, but no plaque or sign identifies its significance. Inside the historical society's building one can ask about the stories of Goody Cole or read through a thick scrapbook detailing her life, her history, and her folklore.

Sometimes it is hard to tell where Eunice's history ends and her folklore begins. As with the Whittier poem, skeptics and critics question what is popularized and "adjusted" to make a better story, and what is truth. First, the Hampton resolution stated they would "hereby *restore* Eunice Cole her rightful place as a citizen of the town of Hampton," but Eunice Cole lived in the 1600s when the idea of a woman having citizenship rights was still centuries away. Second, some in the town may have been concerned about rehabilitating Goody Cole's reputation, but it is interesting to note that the effort happened to fall on the three hundredth anniversary of Hampton's founding. Even the August 25 memorial ceremonies were held as the pivotal event in the town's tricentennial celebration. Newspaper stories about the events in the small resort town gave Hampton a visibility greater than any Chamber of Commerce could dream. Journalists and radio teams came to investigate the story and report on the proceedings. Tourists who heard or read the story continued to visit Hampton long after the speeches were done and the bunting was down. The local economy received a significant boost from the legends and life of Eunice Cole, citizen or not.

Does the reason for all the hoopla matter? Did the citizens of Hampton refuse to say it was not too late and take a stand for fairness, or did they mix fact and folklore into a clever publicity stunt? Whatever the motives, the results are real. The town's resolution sparked conversations about superstition, paranoia, restitution, and justice. Hampton's actions *did* acknowledge a 250-year-old injustice. Hampton became the first community to take official action to right the wrongs of prejudice and superstition that had resulted in so much pain during the early colonial years. Perhaps at last Eunice Cole can rest in peace.

ONA JUDGE STAINES

ca. 1774–1848

George Washington's Fugitive Slave

WALKING THROUGH PORTSMOUTH'S MARKET DISTRICT, Ona Judge may have been going through a mental checklist of supplies she needed. She may have been just enjoying the weather. Whatever Ona was thinking on that day in 1796, those thoughts surely fled her mind when she spotted the familiar face in the crowd. What was Elizabeth Langdon doing here, so many miles from Philadelphia? Had Elizabeth seen her? Would she recognize Ona? It appeared that Elizabeth was about to stop and speak to her. Careful not to give any sign of recognition, Ona quickly brushed past before a conversation could begin or a question could be asked.

President George Washington had signed the Fugitive Slave Act in 1793, three years before Ona fled her master's home to find freedom in New England. If Ona were found, she would be returned to slavery. That was the law. Her fragile but precious freedom would be over. Although her master had treated her well, Ona wanted no master . . . not even a master who was the first president of the new United States.

When Ona Judge was born, her mother, Betty, was a slave at

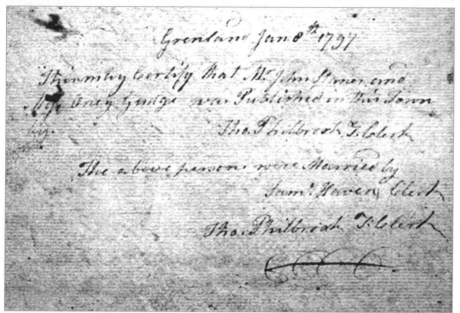

There are no known images of Ona Staines, but this image from the Town of Greenland Vital Records of January 8, 1797, documents the publication of her marriage intentions and her marriage to John Staines.

the Mount Vernon home of George and Martha Washington. Ona's father, Andrew Judge, had come from England in 1772, agreeing to serve four years as a white indentured servant. Betty was a "Dower Negro," having come from the estate of Martha Washington's first husband, Daniel Custis. Under the laws in 1774, children born to slave mothers were considered the property of whoever owned the mother. So, when Andrew Judge finished his indenture in 1776, he became free, but his daughter Ona remained a slave.

Ona was brought to live in the main house when she was only ten years old. She was a convenient playmate for the Washingtons' granddaughter, Nelly Custis, and may have even shared a room with her. More important, Ona was learning to be an attendant for Martha Washington. Betty was a skilled seamstress and passed on her advanced skills in sewing, weaving, spinning, and tailoring to her daughter. Soon Ona was asked to do most of Martha's fine sewing as well as the meticulous preparation of clear-starching, quilling, and frilling Mrs. Washington's hats. The Washingtons later described Ona as "perfect Mistress of her needle."

George Washington was elected the first president of the United States in 1789. That April fifteen-year-old Ona and six other slaves left the Mount Vernon plantation, family and friends, and traveled to New York City to work for the Washingtons in the presidential residence. The following year they moved with the president to the new President's House in Philadelphia. By then Ona was not only Mrs. Washington's seamstress but her personal attendant.

Household account books from those years reflect shopping trips and social events when Ona accompanied Mrs. Washington, buying clothes, traveling to see the circus, and moving about the city of Philadelphia with the Washingtons. Life with the First Family was not exactly a hardship, and Ona had much more freedom of movement than many slaves, but she was still a slave. She had her own room but yearned to learn to read, to write, and to make her own decisions. As a slave Ona had no control over her life and destiny. She was well aware that, as part of their estate, when the Washingtons died she would be left in their will to whomever they chose. Perhaps Ona would be left to their granddaughter Nelly, with whom she had once played. Perhaps she would be a wedding gift to a daughter or other favored relative. But Ona wanted to be free. She certainly had the opportunity in Philadelphia to meet free blacks and probably developed a circle of friends in both the slave and free black communities. Listening to the stories and seeing the lives of both, Ona longed for the independence to determine her own fate.

When Ona learned in May of 1796 that the Washingtons were preparing to move back to Virginia, she knew time was running out.

She had friends among the free blacks in Philadelphia; it would be much harder to escape once the family was back in Virginia. The Washingtons planned to leave for Mount Vernon on Monday, June 13. Ona had to act quickly. She continued to help Mrs. Washington pack the household belongings for the trip, but she also discreetly passed some of her few belongings to friends in the black community so that she could leave more easily when the time came.

One evening, while the Washingtons were eating their dinner, Ona slipped out of the house. She gathered her meager belongings and walked to the docks. She needed to find a captain who was about to head north and who would not ask too many questions about an unaccompanied black woman.

Captain John Bowles captained the *Nancy,* a sloop that sailed between Portsmouth, New Hampshire, and Philadelphia about once a month. The *Nancy* had left Portsmouth in May and was set to return on June 1, 1796, with a load of harnesses, bridles, saddles, and other leather goods to sell in New Hampshire. The *Nancy* made another trip on June 25. Historians aren't sure which trip Ona joined, and she never revealed whether Captain Bowles knew from whom Ona was fleeing. But we do know she sailed to New Hampshire on the *Nancy*. Anyone caught assisting a slave's escape faced severe sentences for "illegal confiscation of property." Secrecy was crucial, and those who helped seldom asked questions or talked about what they had done. Not until Bowles died in 1837 did Ona reveal the name of the man who had allowed her passage to the North.

Arriving in New Hampshire, Ona found safety and a taste of freedom. Like Massachusetts, New Hampshire had a history of providing asylum for runaway slaves. She soon made new friends within Portsmouth's black community. But after seeing Elizabeth Langdon, a frequent visitor at the Washingtons' home, at the market, Ona must have feared that her precious freedom was about to be cut short.

Despite Ona's efforts to slip away in the crowd, Elizabeth Langdon not only saw Ona but recognized her. Elizabeth had seen Ona many times while visiting the Washingtons, and she knew the couple was looking for her. Elizabeth sent word, and by the time George Washington returned to Philadelphia, he knew where Ona was.

Washington was determined to get Ona back. His wife Martha desperately missed Ona's unique skills as a seamstress, as well as everything else Ona had done for her day to day. President Washington appealed to the Portsmouth Collector of Customs, Joseph Whipple, requesting the prompt return of his missing slave girl, Ona Maria Judge, who had been "illegally delivered" to Portsmouth.

On September 1 Washington sent the letter to Whipple via Secretary of the Treasury Oliver Wolcott. Washington said he didn't know if Ona was traveling through Portsmouth or staying there, but he worried that whoever had "enticed" her to leave the Washingtons would try to hide Ona if they knew she had been discovered. He suggested that the safest and least expensive course of action might be "to seize, and put her on board a Vessel bound immediately to this place." Washington offered Miss Langdon to provide proof of Ona's identity and promised reimbursement for any expenses incurred. Showing his irritation with Ona's daring flight, Washington wrote, "the ingratitude of the girl, who was brought up and treated more like a child than a Servant (and Mrs. Washington's desire to recover her) ought not to escape with impunity if it can be avoided."

What happened next is unclear. Ona rarely talked about those years, so her version is missing from the record. Joseph Whipple wrote a brief reply on September 10, 1796, confirming that Ona was living in Portsmouth. A month later he sent a detailed letter to Washington describing his efforts to obtain Ona's return. Whipple reported booking tentative passage on a boat sailing to

Philadelphia and sending for Ona on the ruse of a job interview for a position with his family. He told Washington that Ona had not been lured away, that a "thirst for compleat freedom" had been her only motive. Perhaps to assuage the president, he wrote that "she expressed great affection and reverence for her Master and Mistress," explaining that Ona said she would be happy to return if she could be assured of her freedom upon their death, but that she would rather die than be a slave to be sold or given away.

Whipple wrote that he had tentatively booked passage for Ona sailing to Philadelphia the next day, but a "contrary wind" delayed its departure. During that delay Ona's plans were supposedly discovered by acquaintances who dissuaded her from going back to the Washingtons—and the ship sailed without her. Whether all this really happened or whether Whipple was writing something to pacify his president cannot be determined, but the rest of Whipple's letter let the president know it would not be easy to obtain Ona's return.

Whipple tactfully made it plain that the sentiment in Massachusetts and New Hampshire favored universal freedom, making the forcible return of runaway slaves challenging. Although slavery was still legal in New Hampshire, the population generally objected to it. Repeating that Ona would not return to slavery voluntarily, Whipple suggested that the legal and most effective next step would be through the Attorney of the United States in New Hampshire. Whipple proposed that an "Officer of the President's Household" contact the Attorney to exercise whatever means "authorized by the Constitution of the United States."

Washington's reply was delayed by an extended visit to Mount Vernon, but his next letter of October 4 showed no change in his unwavering desire to obtain Ona's return. He emphatically rejected the idea of allowing Ona to return with the promise of freedom, saying, "To enter into such a compromise with her, as she suggested to you, is totally inadmissible." Washington tried to explain: " . . . however well disposed I might be to a gradual abolition, or even to an entire emancipation of the description of People (if the latter was in itself practicable at this moment) it would neither be politic or just to reward *unfaithfulness* with a premature preference; and thereby discontent beforehand the minds of all her fellow-servants who by their steady attachments are far more deserving than herself of favor."

Apparently still unable or unwilling to believe Ona had escaped of her own volition, Washington went on to describe the family's belief that Ona had been "seduced and enticed off by a Frenchman." He closed the letter with an offer, a threat, and a politically savvy caution. If Ona would return immediately, all would be forgiven and she would again receive the kind treatment her large family already received. If not, he would resort to further measures to put her on board a ship and return her at once. Even so, Washington ruled out any "violent measures used as would excite a mob or riot," showing some awareness of the political sensitivity of his position. Admitting he would rather do without Ona's services than cause "uneasy Sensations in the Minds of well disposed Citizens," he closed with a final plea that Mrs. Washington get her wish to have Ona back.

Washington made no mention of Whipple's suggestion to pursue Ona's return through the legal system. Perhaps he was astute enough to realize that this would be treating Ona, a slave, as if she had the rights of a United States citizen, a precedent likely to have had dangerous, far-reaching repercussions.

Whipple sent his final reply on December 22, 1796. He again expressed regret at his lack of success in returning Ona to Mrs. Washington, knowing how much she valued and missed Ona's services. He again hinted at his feelings regarding what he felt would be a wiser course of action saying, "I conceived that a Servant . . .

returning voluntarily, [is] of infinitely more value in the estimation of her employer than one taken forceably like a felon to punishment." Whipple revealed that his inquiries about Ona had found that she was planning to marry under the applicable New Hampshire laws regarding mulattos. He promised to try to prevent the publishing of her marriage intentions, thus delaying the wedding. Whipple closed with an incongruous mix of a final appeal for the "abolition of this species of servitude" and asserting his hope that his services "in executing your commands" would be acceptable to the president.

How hard Whipple tried we do not know, but on January 8, 1797, Thomas Philbrook, town clerk of Greenland, New Hampshire, recorded: "This may Certify that Mr. John Staines and Miss Ona Judge was Published in this Town." Staines and Ona did not delay. An announcement in the January 14 *Gazette* reported that a Dr. Samuel Haven had performed the marriage ceremony in Portsmouth. Newlyweds Jack and Ona settled in Portsmouth. George Washington handed over the office of president to John Adams on March 4 and with Martha returned to Mount Vernon.

As Portsmouth became home for the newlyweds, they undoubtedly felt an undercurrent of worry, wondering if Washington was still seeking Ona's return. But she enjoyed each day of freedom, and soon they began a family. Two years later, December 1799, like others all across the country, they heard the news. George Washington, who had led the country to independence and served as the first president of the United States, had died on December 14.

As she became older, Ona knew she was less valuable and probably not worth the cost of searching or forcing her return. But legally, Ona remained a fugitive slave. The Washington family was probably unaware that Ona had children. By law any descendents or heirs of Martha Washington held legal claim not only to Ona but also to any of Ona's children. Technically, at any moment slave hunters could kidnap her or her children and return them to the Washington family and a life of slavery. Since the Washington family knew that she was in New Hampshire, there must have been a part of Ona that continued to worry for her children, if not for herself.

Ona and Jack Staines had three children: William, Eliza, and Nancy. Ona learned to read and made connections with a church community in Portsmouth. Jack died in 1803, just six years after marrying Ona, who was left with three small children. Ona continued to live in Portsmouth for a time, working as a live-in maid for the Bartlett family. The black community of Portsmouth was a dependable source of moral support and practical help as Ona worked to raise her children. Her son William became a sailor and was assumed lost at sea when his ship failed to return from a voyage in the 1820s. Daughters Eliza and Nancy worked in a variety of New Hampshire homes as servants but also earned money from their artistic talents. The girls drew and sold pen and pencil sketches later framed under glass and hung in Greenland homes. Some of their sketches bore phrases such as "I had both Ona and a friend" and were drawn over and over as often as they could be sold. Like their brother, both girls died in their twenties.

With neither husband nor children to help support her as she grew older, Ona moved back to Greenland, New Hampshire, and lived with the Jacks family. The death of Phyllis Jacks left two daughters, Nancy and Phyllis Jr., to take care of the aging John Jacks. Ona was able to help with the garden and with housework. This arrangement continued for many years. A pauper, Ona eventually received support from the town of Greenland. Records detail yearly donations of firewood, food, and other needed supplies. She also received gifts from visitors.

Ona was a bit of a local celebrity. Visitors curious about the woman who had once been a slave in the home of the president would stop by to visit with her. Ona would receive them graciously and happily accept their presents of food and supplies. One of her last interviews was with the Reverend Benjamin Chase. Ona told the story of her flight to New Hampshire, of the president's attempts to have her returned, and of the end of those attempts when Washington died. Her story appeared in the *Granite Freeman* on May 22, 1845, and again, in a letter to the editor, in the famous abolitionist paper the *Liberator* on January 1, 1847.

Ona Judge Staines died February 25, 1848, and was buried in a small family plot on the Jacks' land. Two hundred fifty years later, that plot is evident only by a few broken stone markers almost obscured by overgrown grasses, weeds, and fallen trees.

A New Hampshire interviewer had once asked Ona if she had any regrets. Ona answered, "No, I am free, and have, I trust, been made a child of God by the means."

Ona left a comfortable life as Martha Washington's favorite maid—and in New Hampshire she faced extreme hardship. But in New Hampshire she married a man of her own choosing. She kept her family together as she chose. She learned to read and write. She had control of her own time and chose her own hobbies.

In the eyes of the law, however, Ona Judge Staines was a slave until the day she died.

Growing up in George Washington's household, Ona heard about freedom and tried to imagine it. But she was not satisfied with hearing or dreaming. Despite the risks, she defied the president of the United States and fled. With courageous action and steadfast determination she claimed and built a life of freedom in New Hampshire. Ona won choice. Ona chose freedom.

SARAH JOSEPHA HALE

1788–1879

Publishing Pioneer

SARAH MOVED QUICKLY ABOUT THE ROOM, putting everything in its place and checking that all was ready for the next day. Though of average height, she was slim and walked with such an erect posture that she appeared taller. Self-contained and graceful, Sarah maintained an air of dignity even when excited.

Almost ready for bed, Sarah reached into the dresser drawer, took out a sheet of heavy brown butcher paper, cut off several pieces, and dipped them in a bowl of fresh apple vinegar. Her small, white hands carefully applied each piece to the temples of her broad forehead to prevent any crow's feet from marring her fair, smooth complexion. Next she reached for the bottle of hand lotion she kept on the dressing table. It was her own recipe of rosewater, coconut milk, and lard, and she kept a bottle at the sink, dressing table, even her desk. Each time Sarah washed her hands or felt any hint of roughness, she applied the lotion immediately. Finally ready, she climbed into bed, read her Bible, and turned out the lamp.

Sarah gave every appearance of a thirty-something lady of leisure preparing for sleep before a day of society gatherings and

This engraving, used in *Godey's Lady's Book*, shows Sarah Josepha Hale in 1850 at age sixty-two, but looking far younger.

afternoon teas. Hardly. The next day fifty-two-year-old Sarah Hale would set aside her "routine" duties as literary editor of America's largest women's magazine. For each of the next seven days Sarah would research, write, print, and distribute a four-page newspaper covering a literally monumental project. She had been working for months on a fund-raising plan to save the stalled Bunker Hill Monument construction.

The weeklong craft fair at Boston's Quincy Hall was Sarah's brainchild and, if successful, might save the monument. The monument's cornerstone had been laid with great fanfare and oratory in 1825. Since then construction of the 221-foot obelisk design had been suspended twice, first with 40 feet complete, and now at 80 feet. The first time construction was suspended Sarah had asked each of her magazine's readers to send one dollar. But far more was needed now. At Sarah's urging, women all over New England had crafted jewelry, quilts, baskets, and needlework. They had preserved jams and jellies and baked all manner of pies and cakes. They had obtained autographs of George Washington, the Marquis de Lafayette, and James Madison to sell, and had solicited donations of books, amulets, portfolios—even a piano.

After two months of nonstop effort, everything was organized, every table stocked, and the fair would finally open in the morning. Sarah's father had fought in the Revolutionary War, and many of those who fought in the Battle of Bunker Hill had been from her beloved home state of New Hampshire. Sarah desperately wanted the monument completed, and for that she knew the fair must be a success.

Born October 23, 1788, Sarah Josepha Hale was the third of four children. She grew up near Newport, New Hampshire, on a four-hundred-acre East Mountain family farm overlooking Sugar River. Her father Gordon, wounded in the Revolutionary War, filled the children with stories of heroes and battles in the great fight for independence. Her mother Martha filled them with the stories of the Bible, Milton, Pope, and Shakespeare, tutoring the children daily. Sarah always adored her one-year-older brother Horatio, and when he gained admission to Dartmouth College, in Hanover, New Hampshire, a two-day journey by stage, she waited eagerly for each return.

While Horatio was at Dartmouth, Sarah began teaching school. Other than an occasional elderly widow or spinster, most teachers were men, and the education they offered was rigid and limited. Girls were taught the alphabet but then educated only in sewing, cooking, embroidery, samplers, and such. Boys automatically progressed to math, literature, and advanced studies. Students moved through prescribed lessons, learning by group recitation. Sarah, on the other hand, avoided group recitations and allowed students to move at their own pace. Far more radical, Sarah insisted that even the girls learn practical math, to read for pleasure and knowledge, and to write competently.

Every time Horatio returned on break, he tutored Sarah in each of his courses. Keeping study hours as regular as college classes, Sarah covered philosophy, math, even Latin. By the time Horatio graduated at the top of his Dartmouth class, Sarah had gained the closest equivalent to a college education available to a woman.

Teaching privately in small villages, Sarah was a well-respected and successful teacher. After seven years, and still unmarried at twenty-five, Sarah would have been considered an old maid. By then her father's health had deteriorated, and unable to manage the farm, he moved the family into Newport and opened a small tavern, The Rising Sun. There, in 1811, Sarah met a young lawyer recently arrived in Newport to open a law practice. David Hale was quickly smitten by the strikingly beautiful schoolteacher with hazel eyes, long thick lashes, and slow smile. He and Sarah began courting and on October 23, 1813, were married at The Rising Sun.

The Hales' marriage was remarkable and happy. Universally admired, David was active in the town, church, and Masons. He had a keen mind and encouraged his wife to explore and expand hers as well. Sarah later described their evenings.

> We commenced, soon after our marriage, a system of study and reading . . . The hours allotted were from eight o'clock until ten—two hours in each twenty-four. How I enjoyed those hours! In this manner we studied French, Botany . . . and obtained some knowledge of Mineralogy, Geology, etc. besides pursuing a long and instructive course of readings.

Every evening ended with reading from the Bible before they went to bed.

The Hales' evening ritual continued even as their family grew. First came David in 1815 and two years later Horatio. In the fall of 1818, when Sarah was pregnant with their third child, she became seriously ill. Doctors believed it was "quick consumption," or tuberculosis, for which there was no cure. Soon Sarah appeared to give up. The family later passed down the story of a night David stopped reading aloud to Sarah, closed his book, and left the house. Some hours later he returned and announced he was *not* going to let Sarah die. The next morning he took the two boys to stay with Sarah's brothers and set off with her. For six weeks they meandered through the countryside in an open carriage, stopping and eating at whim, enjoying the balmy fall weather, fresh air, and sunshine. Sarah particularly loved the grapes that grew wild along the road, and they would stop to gather and eat them at every opportunity. When they returned to Newport, Sarah had regained her health. For the rest of her life Sarah kept grapes on her table, even when only hothouse grapes were available.

Daughters Frances and Sarah expanded the family in 1819 and 1820, but the pattern of life remained constant. The Hales began a literary club that met in their Main Street home, and David encouraged Sarah's interest in writing. He offered to critique her prose and persuaded her to submit pieces for publication. David's legal practice was growing, and they were enjoying a prosperous life of intellectual exploration and loving devotion. Sarah later called these nine years a time of "unbroken happiness."

Sarah was expecting a fifth child in the fall of 1822 when her world collapsed. On September 25, David Hale died unexpectedly of pneumonia. Just days later, William was born. Despite David's success, they had not yet begun putting money aside. Sarah was suddenly a heartbroken, thirty-four-year-old widow with five children under the age of eight and no income to support them.

David's Masonic friends helped with burial costs and his sister Hannah invited Sarah to join her in opening a millinery shop. Somehow, between sewing hats and parenting, Sarah returned to the writing she had enjoyed with David. The Masons helped her publish a collection of her poems that enjoyed modest success. By 1825 Sarah began to be published regularly in the *Boston Spectator,* the *American Monthly Magazine,* and the *United States Literary Gazette.* Her poems, essays, and short stories periodically won monetary prizes in literary competitions. Sarah started serious work on a novel titled *Northwood* in hopes of earning support for her family. She later recalled it was "written literally with my baby in my arms."

Northwood is considered the first novel to use American national life as its background, and it dealt with the question of slavery almost twenty-five years before Harriet Beecher Stowe's *Uncle Tom's Cabin.* Published in America in 1827, it was also printed and sold successfully in England. *Northwood* won Sarah Hale critical praise and gained her entrance to the literary world.

Among the many letters of praise Sarah received after *Northwood* was one from a Reverend John Blake. He asked Sarah to move to Boston and edit the *Ladies' Magazine,* the first American literary work geared exclusively for women. Publishing was a risky business, offering no guaranteed income for young men, much less mothers of five. Nonetheless, forty-year-old Sarah found the courage to accept. On her first editorial page, Sarah wrote: "Our doubts are traitors, and make us lose the good we oft might win, by fearing to attempt." Sarah moved past her "fearing to attempt," past her doubts, and became the first female editor of a major American magazine. The good Sarah would accomplish was just beginning.

Reverend Blake taught Sarah the skills of text preparation and the mechanics of publishing, but Sarah defined the magazine's journalistic mission, "to educate and enlighten readers, not merely entertain them." The public accepted her, partly because of her literary reputation, and probably also out of respect for a widow working to support her young children. What started as curiosity quickly led to loyal subscribers, and in barely two years Sarah went from an unknown New England milliner to a literary personage of growing stature.

For ten years Sarah edited the *Ladies' Magazine,* putting her own stamp on the world of women's periodicals. "My first object, in assuming my position was to promote the education of my own sex," she stated. Not satisfied to entertain her readers, Sarah threaded every issue with articles that strove "to improve the female character." She worked for social changes, such as an essay on duels that challenged readers to make the practice "unfashionable" and led to its demise. She featured book reviews and poetry from the leading writers of the day, particularly seeking out female writers. Sarah wanted to celebrate what was distinctively American, even changing the name in 1834 to the *American Ladies' Magazine.* She insisted that stories include American plants, animals, people, and places, and American women flocked to read it all. From the beginning Sarah often wrote at least half of each issue. Readers' letters, question and answer columns, series about schooling, family development, and temperance . . . very little escaped her editorial attention.

Despite editorial demands, Sarah continued to write poetry, sometimes even for other magazines or collections. Educator Lowell Mason asked Sarah to write some poems he could set to music for schoolchildren. She published a small paperback, *Poems for Our Children*, and its 1830 publication is the earliest known printing of the poem "Mary's Lamb," more commonly known as "Mary Had a Little Lamb." Years later some question whether Sarah wrote all of the poem or only part of it, but most research supports Sarah as sole author. She also wrote and edited collections of fiction for young readers, edited a ten-volume *Little Boys' and Girls' Library*, and attempted a children's magazine, *Juvenile Miscellany*.

Sarah also found other ways to benefit children. Boston Harbor in the 1830s was a hectic seaport with up to 1,500 ships sailing annually. Sarah's brother Charles had been a seafarer, and she was acutely aware of the difficult economic conditions for their families. She identified with women left alone to raise their children during long voyages or when a husband was lost at sea, and she helped found the Seamen's Aid Society, the first in the United States, in 1833. Through the society, Sarah organized schooling for the children—academics in the morning, skills and culture in the afternoon. Instead of charity, she fought for employment at fair rates that recognized women's skills in domestics and needlework, and she advocated for clean, low-rent housing.

Sarah never let her charitable work and social activism hurt her magazine, which continued to grow in popularity. Subscriptions climbed, but Sarah always struggled with the economics of a magazine. In the difficult times of the 1830s, one of her primary literary competitors proposed an opportunity. Louis Godey, founder of the Philadelphia-based *Godey's Lady's Book,* admired Sarah's work and wanted to hire her. After some negotiations, Godey announced to his readers the upcoming merger with Hale's *American Ladies' Magazine*. The 1836 merger allowed Sarah to focus on literary aspects of editorship and leave the business side entirely to Godey. However, she insisted on editing the magazine from Boston while her youngest son, William, finished Harvard.

Editing a new venture from such a distance was a challenge, but it didn't prevent Sarah from coming to the aid of the Bunker Hill project. When the memorial had stalled, Sarah immediately marshaled her old and new readers to the fight. Sarah need not have worried that night about her fundraiser. The months of work and preparation paid off. On the craft fair's first day, four thousand people attended, topped by more than twelve thousand the next. The seven-day women's fair netted more than thirty thousand dollars, and construction resumed. Three years later the monument was dedicated, again with fanfare and oratories, but Sarah was not there. William had graduated, and Sarah had finally relocated to *Godey's* Pennsylvania headquarters.

Godey's Lady's Book was known even then for its beautiful fashion plate pages. Realizing they increased magazine sales, Sarah tolerated the fashion pages but insisted that at least half of the magazine's content be literary. She continued to actively promote American writers, especially women, by publishing quality submissions and through her "Book Table" columns. She reviewed the newest literature of the day—poetry, prose, and nonfiction—holding high standards and unafraid to be blunt. Edgar Allen Poe, Frances Hodgson (Burnett), and Harriet Beecher (Stowe) were among those who got their earliest favorable reviews from Sarah. She recommended books and even ran a yearlong series in 1847 that thousands of readers followed. Sarah wanted the magazine to help women seek and achieve "a more respectable station in social life than merely that of household drudge or pretty trifler."

Sarah filled the nonliterary half of *Godey's* with sections for everything from children, etiquette, homemaking, and decorating, to recipes, gardening, patterns, and house plans. Even then, she managed to find ways to innovate. "What a shame we have no *American* fashion to exhibit," Sarah said, then prodded readers to stop imitating Europe and develop their own style. On health pages Sarah supported medical training for women, asserting that since women traditionally cared for the sick, why not educate them, thereby improving the quality of care? Sarah always backed her editorial challenges with personal action. She helped launch the first female medical college in Philadelphia and the Philadelphia Ladies Medical Missionary Society. She assisted in the foundation of Vassar College and urged hiring female instructors. Baltimore Female College awarded Sarah a medal in 1860 "for her distinguished services in the cause of female education."

Education was not Sarah's only cause, nor were all serious. In 1845 she wrote about the new polka dance craze, printing instructions and music for readers to try. She coined the term "Domestic Science" and dared inventors to develop work-saving devices. She trumpeted the invention of the sewing machine and cheerily greeted the ice-cream freezer. In 1853 she issued a challenge for someone to create the first practical clothes washer by the next year.

Regardless of her other priorities, Sarah always made time for patriotism, both personal and national. In 1841 she traveled more than four hundred miles to share a Fourth of July hometown celebration in Newport, New Hampshire, on its eightieth anniversary. Sarah had assisted with the town history and written song lyrics for the occasion, and that day she listened to speeches and readings of the Declaration of Independence and her "Gathering Song."

When Sarah heard in 1855 that George Washington's Mount Vernon home was being sold, she took action. America was struggling with growing divisions, and Sarah believed that saving the first president's home as a national museum might help build a sense of national pride and unity. As with the Bunker Hill campaign, she turned to her readers, inviting donations and printing a list of names and contributions in each issue. Again her campaign was successful. After five years the last payment was made, and the March 1860 magazine announced: "Mount Vernon now belongs to the American nation," purchased by the Vernon Ladies Association.

Mount Vernon was saved, but no campaign, no museum, could stop the divisions that led to the Civil War. Louis Godey was content with Sarah's campaigns for national monuments, but taking a position on war was unthinkable. Godey always held two taboos for his magazine—no sectarian religion and no partisan politics. The magazine's pages never acknowledged the war that was raging. Godey let *Harper's Weekly* and others cover the war, while *Godey's* continued to focus on literature, patterns, household information, and fashion. In the process *Godey's* lost one-third of its circulation.

The magazine's lack of response to the war hurt subscriptions, but the war may have spurred President Abraham Lincoln to help Sarah achieve a long-held personal dream. Beginning in 1846 Sarah had crusaded in *Godey's,* written to magazines and newspapers, and implored every state governor for support. She wanted the New England tradition of a day of giving thanks to become a standardized national celebration. This, she said, was "one of the strongest wishes of my heart." Sarah loved the idea of families gathering to give thanks, enjoying both companionship and the fruits of their labors. As early as one of the *Northwood* chapters, she had included a thanksgiving day in many of her stories and articles. By 1852 twenty-nine states had proclaimed a Thanksgiving on the last Thursday in November. Sarah wanted more. She wanted a presidential proclamation. Sarah lobbied Presidents Polk, Taylor, Fillmore, Pierce, and Buchanan. None was persuaded. Sarah asked her readers to join in lobbying Lincoln. At last, in 1863, President Lincoln issued the proclamation for a national Thanksgiving Day.

Sarah never lost the excitement of a new cause, patriotic, social, feminist, or charitable. Apparently neither did readers, time and time again responding to Sarah's editorials and columns with waves of donations. Given her readership, even small donations mounted up. *Godey's* circulation was ten thousand at the merger and forty thousand just two years later. Between 1837 and 1849 the magazine grew from 48 pages to 100, and in 1860 boasted 150,000 subscribers. Many of the social reforms Sarah advocated, such as infant nutrition, exercise for both boys and girls, playgrounds, kindergartens, sanitation, female doctors and missionaries, expanded job fields and property rights for women, and policies protecting children, seem commonplace now.

One social reform movement Sarah did *not* support was women's suffrage. Sarah advocated the "secret, silent influence of women," suggesting women work behind the scenes, sway the votes of grown men, raise sons to vote based on attitudes with which they were raised, and raise daughters to continue the cycle of influence.

Despite her views on voting, Sarah championed women daily by the causes she supported and by her unwavering commitment to encouraging and celebrating women's achievements. She collected and edited *The Poet's Anthology,* the first collection of women's poetry. Her largest single accolade to women was an encyclopedic biography project completed in 1853. After years of research, correspondence, writing, and editing, Sarah published *Women's Record: or Sketches of All Distinguished Women, from Creation to A.D. 1654.* Divided into four eras, the volume contained 2,500 biographies, 230 portraits, and many samples of writing. Sarah wrote, "My object was to prepare a comprehensive and accurate record of what women have accomplished, in spite of disadvantages of their positions, and to illustrate the great truth that woman's mission is to educate and ameliorate humanity."

Sarah knew those disadvantages. She had experienced the challenges of second-hand education, widowhood, single parenting, and poverty. She always advocated economic independence for women. She may not have foreseen a day when women might *choose* to work, but she knew all women might at some point *need* to work. She endorsed Emma Willard's pleas that "women provide themselves with resources against a day of change."

Sarah's day of change had come without warning, leaving her to raise five children alone. Her life as a housewife who read voraciously at night and occasionally wrote poems or stories ended abruptly. Thanks to her mother, then brother, then husband, Sarah had opportunities for an unusual education. Because Sarah embraced each of those opportunities, when her day of change arrived Sarah *had* provided herself with resources.

Sarah Hale never forgot her beloved David. She always styled her brown hair, which never grayed, in the popular 1820s side curls he had loved. She dressed in simple black the rest of her life, celebrated every wedding anniversary, and delighted in telling their children and grandchildren about him. Early in her editorial career, Sarah described David's dreams for her. "In all our mental pursuits, it seemed the aim of my husband to enlighten my reason, strengthen my judgment, and give me confidence in my own powers of mind, which he estimated more highly than I did." But even David could never have predicted the impact his wife would have on women, on children, and on American culture.

Sarah lived to see a glimmer of her impact on American life and was both humble and proud. In August 1873 Sarah wrote a friend, "In truth, my life is a continuous thanksgiving." Four years later, at age eighty-nine, Sarah retired after fifty years editing magazines for women. That same year Thomas Edison spoke the opening lines of "Mary's Lamb," the first words ever recorded, on his new phonograph machine. Sarah wrote a poem to read at her ninetieth birthday party that began: "Growing old! Growing old! Do they say that of *me?*" Sarah Josepha Hale died at ninety-one in 1879.

When we climb the Bunker Hill Monument, visit Mount Vernon, gather to celebrate Thanksgiving, or hear a child sing about Mary's lamb, we honor Sarah Hale's vision. When we join a stirring debate on education, women's opportunities, or the challenges of single parenting, we echo her leadership. One biographer described Sarah as "a conservative mind animated by a radical spirit." Sarah Hale was a nineteenth-century woman who raised and fought for ideas that still challenge the twenty-first century.

HARRIET LIVERMORE

1788-1868

Evangelist and "Pilgrim Preacher"

"HE THAT RULETH OVER MEN MUST BE JUST, ruling in the fear of God." Harriet's voice was soft but clear, and her enunciation so distinct that each word could be heard in the farthest corner of Congress Hall. Female preachers were a novelty, but Harriet was not unknown. She had visited Washington, D.C., often in her youth, and her family was well known in political and social circles. She had preached in nearby Georgetown and several Washington churches recently, but this Sunday morning sermon promised to be particularly exciting.

Only once before had a woman addressed the men of Congress—English evangelist Dorothy Ripley twenty-one years earlier. This morning in January 1827, with the permission of the Speaker of the House, Harriet Livermore became the first American woman to preach there. The room was overflowing with a mix of the curious and the powerful. The Secretary of War, most of the members of Congress, and even President John Quincy Adams sat eager to hear the female evangelist some had known previously as a lively young socialite.

This engraving is used in most publications by or about
Harriet Livermore.

Harriet entered the room promptly at 11:00 a.m., pleased to see the chambers so crowded. After leading a hymn and offering a prayer, Harriet read 2 Samuel 23:3–4, a somewhat daring text, but beautiful: "He that ruleth over men must be just, ruling in the fear of God. And he shall be as the light of the morning, when the sun riseth, even a morning without clouds: as the tender grass springing out of the earth by clear shining after rain."

Looking out at the congressional leaders among the crowd, Harriet began to preach, detailing the character and attributes of a fair ruler. Point by point she expounded on the good that such a ruler could accomplish in America. During the sermon, President Adams moved closer to the Speaker's chair pulpit, sitting on the steps below where Harriet spoke. Harriet Livermore's build may have been slight, her voice soft and controlled, but her words were powerful. Over and over, Harriet repeated the scriptural directive, boldly charging her listeners to be just.

After more than an hour, Harriet concluded her discourse and closed the service by singing a softly beautiful hymn. One lady in the audience wrote her daughter describing the closing: "I should say she is the most eloquent preacher . . . But no language can do justice to the pathos of her singing. For when she closed by singing a hymn that might with propriety be termed a prayer . . . her voice was so melodious, and her face beamed with such heavenly good-ness as to resemble a transfiguration."

Also in the audience was a man who had known Harriet before her conversion to religious life. He wrote to a New Hamp-shire paper describing his reaction to the event:

She is now past 35 years of age, and retains much of the good looks of her youth. I remember her, when in the blooming charms of seventeen, she moved down the dance "with fairy step and laughing eye:" but little then did I anticipate the day when she would draw after her crowds of hearers as a preacher. I think she will do much good.

That writer was not alone. Few who knew Harriet Livermore as a girl could have predicted the course of her life. However, many years before Harriet preached that morning at Congress Hall in her late-thirties, she had undergone a remarkable transformation into the fervently religious evangelist and self-proclaimed "Pilgrim Preacher."

Harriet Livermore had been born into a family of intelligence, wealth, and political involvement. Her grandfather, Samuel Livermore, was a respected judge and attorney general. Her father Edward, also a lawyer, seemed destined for politics as well. Edward moved the family to Concord, New Hampshire, shortly after passing the bar exam, and it was in Concord that Harriet was born on April 14, 1788. Her father was known for being a fair and honest man, albeit sometimes a bit hotheaded. Harriet was one of five children, and whatever her upbringing might have been changed forever just before Harriet was five, when her mother died at age twenty-eight.

Harriet quickly became a difficult child. She survived the trauma of losing her mother, then being raised mostly by nannies, and finally a difficult relationship with a disliked stepmother when Edward remarried. In the process, Harriet developed a disposition that by all accounts was volatile at best. On one hand, Harriet could be extremely generous and thoughtful, but, on the other hand, she might fly into a tantrum or lash out in a rage.

By the time Harriet was eight, her father had sent her to a boarding school in Haverhill, New Hampshire, followed by Byfield Female Seminary in Massachusetts and the Atkinson Academy, back in New Hampshire. Keeping Harriet in private schools avoided confrontations in the family but did little to smooth her temper. Outwardly, Harriet led a pampered and proper life. She attended the best schools, took dancing lessons, and spent hours of ladylike leisure playing cards. Commenting on the personality that lay beneath the social exterior, Harriet later wrote, "I was never endued with any natural equanimity, moderation, or sweetness. . . . I was always called passionate from my earliest remembrance." Whether it was labeled passion, emotion, or temper, Harriet's volatility may have cost her a completely different life. While at the Atkinson Academy, Harriet became close to a young man and marriage seemed likely. However, both families were opposed to the marriage, and some sources hint that her beau's family was concerned about whether Harriet's "tempestuous nature" was suitable for married life. Whatever the reasons, the marriage never took place.

Harriet had other opportunities to meet people. Harriet's father had become a judge, then a justice on the New Hampshire Supreme Court, and her grandfather represented New Hampshire in the United States Senate from 1793 to 1801. The Livermore family moved in the social worlds of politics and wealth, both in New Hampshire and in Washington. Harriet's father moved to Massachusetts in 1816 and soon was running for the House of Representatives, where he eventually served three terms. When Harriet visited her family in Washington, she easily found a place in society.

In social gatherings Harriet stood out. Set against her fair complexion, Harriet's dark eyes were often described as "luminous" and were matched by dark, silky hair more than three feet long, which swirled around Harriet's delicate frame as she danced. No wonder that years later one man recalled Harriet's "blooming charm" as she "moved down the dance with fairy step and laughing eye." Attractive, intelligent, wealthy, and socially connected, she caught the attention of society pages. One letter printed in the Haverhill paper described the "gracefulness with which the beautiful Harriet

Livermore tripped to and fro, in the 'Merry Dance,' among the Elite of Washington."

Despite her vivacious appearance, Harriet was inwardly restless, unhappy, and alone. She had no prospects for marriage in an age when marriage was the most common and acceptable path for women. Some believed Harriet never got over her one lost love. Whatever the reason, Harriet seemed unable to settle down and find a place in life.

At twenty-three, Harriet made a surprising decision. Describing it later, she said: "I drew up a resolution in my mind to commence a religious life—to become a religious person." Not motivated by "fears of hell, nor desires for Heaven" but rather "as a present sanctuary from the sorrows of life . . . It is very probably, had my lot been cast in some part of Europe, instead of America, I should have immured myself within the walls of a cloister." But from a Baptist family and in the more open, independent world of America, Harriet determined to become a female preacher.

In the early 1800s a woman's participation in the ministry was extremely limited. Many considered religious life a last resort for the unattractive or unskilled, not a vocation for a young woman with Harriet's looks, wealth, or intelligence. For a woman who wished to preach, the challenges were even greater. A few female evangelists had emerged, but it was a difficult path. In May 1817 Harriet wrote a friend: "[I] am sensible that trials await me everywhere, while sojourning in this vale of tears, and therefore do not expect happiness without alloy, till my spirit is at rest in Jesus' bosom, beyond the skies."

Baptized as an infant, and confirmed by an Episcopal bishop at fourteen, Harriet began exploring to find a spiritual home. She tried the Congregationalists, Quakers, Presbyterians, and more, until in October 1821 she was baptized by immersion into the Baptist Church. With typical intensity Harriet transformed her physical appearance, cutting her hair and trading her fashionable clothes for plain, somber frocks and a simple bonnet. Then, with single-minded purpose, Harriet set out into the world and began to evangelize.

Harriet had no formal sponsorship and so had to find her own opportunities to preach. She later wrote that over the next decade she "preached among Presbyterians, Episcopals, Methodists, and Dunkers, also at the Magdalen House, Widows Asylum and the Prison." Unlike some of the more radical women evangelists, Harriet's conservative theology made it easier for her to be welcomed by the male clergy who would often loan her their pulpits and write recommendations for her. She was unintimidated by crowds of sailors on the Philadelphia wharves and fearless "standing before five hundred miserable devotees to vice" in the prison wards. Free Will Baptists, Dunkers, Millerites, German Brethren, camp meetings . . . Harriet traveled from one to another, stopping only when exhaustion required rest. Sometimes the offerings and the support of her listeners made travel by stagecoach possible. When money was scarce, Harriet was undeterred and traveled on foot, day after day, to her next destination. For years Harriet carried a collection of her mother's silver spoons, selling them one at a time when finances dictated.

Harriet quickly became known in religious circles and, by the 1820s, she achieved near-celebrity status among evangelists. Crowds of people would flock to the woman known for her powerful preaching and beautiful songs. When the opportunity came to speak in Congress Hall, Harriet was ready.

Soon after her 1827 sermon in Congress Hall, Harriet made her first pilgrimage to the Holy Land. Still relatively unknown outside the United States, Harriet enjoyed the anonymity. Without the attention she drew at home, Harriet was free to explore the places and sights so familiar to her from the Bible. After returning to

Philadelphia, she stayed for a while with another New Hampshire native, poet John Greenleaf Whittier. Whittier helped Harriet find audiences for lectures about her Holy Land travels, earning up to $150 per lecture. Harriet also continued to publish her hymns and writings, which helped finance her work.

On May 27, 1832, Harriet returned to the Capitol and again led a spirited Sunday worship in the Congress Hall. Massachusetts congressman George N. Briggs, later governor, wrote:

> I attended church at the Capitol this morning, and heard the celebrated Harriet Livermore, of New Hampshire, preach. . . . She is, without exception, the sweetest singer I ever heard. Her voice is inconceivably sweet, and though not loud, was distinctly heard by probably a thousand people, and every word was perfectly articulated. She said she was going among the Indians . . .

Harriet headed west with a new cause. Native Americans were losing their land, being forced to endure long, devastating marches to reservations, and were slaughtered in battles scattered along the frontiers. Much of this was happening at the hands of the U.S. government. Harriet explained her hopes later, saying:

> I left these States in 1832, to seek for the poor sheep in the wilderness; and from a heart aching with sympathy for wrongs and sorrows which I could not remedy, to pour out the tributary stream of pity and affection, on the altar of prayer to the Indian's God.

Harriet set off through the wilderness settlements to the frontier territories for what became three years. Undaunted by the dangers, she traveled thousands of miles alone at a time when women traveled such routes only in the company of a husband, family, or as part of a missionary's group. Other missionaries to the Indians had the blessing and support of a denomination, but in all ways and by choice, Harriet was alone, "conscientiously solitary" in her journey.

Harriet traveled from tribe to tribe, gaining their respect as she shared her message of faith and preached of the new day coming. She became known by the Indians for treating them with a sense of equality and fairness. The Osage tribe gave her the nickname "Wahconda's Wakko"—God's woman. Soon Harriet began to believe the Indians were more than just a beleaguered people. She came to believe the Native Americans were the famed Lost Tribe of Israel, and her attitude toward them became one of almost reverence. Not surprisingly, the Bureau of Indian Affairs was determined to stop Harriet's work. When heading to work with natives in the Kansas Territory, Harriet was turned back at Fort Leavenworth, Kansas.

Taking a different tack, Harriet returned to the East and wrote *The Harp of Israel, to Meet the Loud Echo in the Wilds of America.* Published in 1835, it included a chart comparing similar words and phrases in Hebrew and Indian languages as part of her argument that Indians were the Lost Tribes. Most of the book was filled with hymns that Harriet had written "as a testimony of immortal and eternal friendship, for the afflicted red men." In a letter to Cherokee Indian editor Elias Boudinot, Harriet told her dreams for the hymns, even while admitting the likely hopelessness:

O! could I realize, that the murmuring breeze of the forests in Missouri, would mingle with my simple songs, repeated by the Christian Kickappoo, or Potawattamie Indians, in their sorrowful days, my praisings to God should ascend on the wings of the morning, on the cloud of the evening, in strains of adoring gratitude, that he permitted me to write them. But alas! I fear this joy may never be mine. Those tribes know not the white man's language.

Harriet's views on the Indians combined with her growing conviction that the time of the Second Coming was near. "Believing the glorious epiphany, and personal reign of the Lord Jesus Christ very near at hand, when the children of the forest, the Aborigines of America shall enter their holy rest," Harriet decided to return to the Holy Land. She eventually made five trips to Jerusalem, each time enduring harsh conditions, illness, and financial struggles. She hoped to be there for the Second Coming, once stating, "I go forward to meet my lot, which, I fervently hope, is martyrdom at last, in Jerusalem, the ancient city of God." Between trips she spoke where she could, wrote and published rambling letters and treatises, and preached in Congress Hall again in 1838 and 1843. But the most renowned female evangelist in the country gradually became estranged from the people who once flocked to hear her.

Harriet's fame of the previous decades was being overshadowed by the growing women's movement. The 1848 women's rights convention in Seneca Falls made Susan B. Anthony and Elizabeth Cady Stanton prominent figures, but Harriet had no interest in political action. Despite the topic of her first book, *Scriptural Evidence in Favor of Female Testimony,* Harriet never advocated for ordination of women, nor for women in a leadership role. Once a groundbreaker, Harriet now seemed to be left behind.

At age seventy-seven Harriet planned her final trip to the Holy Land. She was more frail and more eccentric than ever. Her last book, *Thoughts on Important Subjects,* had just been published in 1864 but had brought in little money, certainly not enough for her passage or expenses. Harriet reached out to influential acquaintances to sponsor the journey. John Quincy Adams, John Tyler, and Mrs. James Madison were among those who paid to "subscribe" to Harriet's next book. As there was no formal plan for a next book, nor evidence that they had purchased (much less read) her previous books, this was likely a form of gracious charity rather than real interest.

One final time Harriet walked the streets of Jerusalem preparing for the Second Coming. Again there was no apocalypse. No chariot. No Day of Judgment . . . only increasingly bizarre behavior. The powerful preacher, who moved audiences with her words and her songs, was now reported walking the olive groves outside Jerusalem demanding money for the Great King from passersby. Harriet was forced to return home.

Having spent what little she had for that last trip, Harriet was now totally dependent on the kindness of others. There were no more books, no preaching tours, no speaking engagements. Never having been affiliated with a particular denomination, she had no church structure to provide charity in her old age. Friends and relatives in the Philadelphia area helped, but for the most part Harriet was alone. She turned further and further inward and became increasingly more eccentric. Harriet began a descent into obscurity.

In 1866 New Hampshire poet John Greenleaf Whittier published the book *Snowbound.* It sold so well that Whittier became wealthy. Livermore family legend says that when Harriet first read the description of her in *Snowbound,* she threw the book across the room in fury. Whittier describes Harriet's eccentricities, choosing words to paint an unflattering, even intimidating picture. Whittier labels her appearance as "a not un-feared, half-welcome guest." He describes her differing personalities of "vixen" and "devotee" and her unpredictable mood swings:

> Her tapering hand and rounded wrist
> Had facile power to form a fist;
> The warm, dark languish of her eyes
> Was never safe from wrath's surprise.

In all likelihood, the popularity of *Snowbound* and its image of Harriet Livermore had little impact on her legacy. She had long ago lost the support of traditional evangelical groups as the beliefs she preached became more radical and her lifestyle more bizarre. The celebrity status of the 1820s and 1830s was gone. The crowds no longer came.

Years before, Harriet had chosen a solitary life. Despite her travels, speaking, and writing, Harriet neither developed a close circle of friends nor maintained close connections with her remaining family. As an old woman, Harriet's solitary life left her isolated yet unable to manage alone. Behavior once considered unconventional became behavior that others viewed as deranged. Harriet spent the end of her life in a Philadelphia boarding house for the poor. On March 30, 1868, Harriet Livermore died without money even for burial expenses. No grand funeral drew crowds, no articles or lofty obituaries mourned the pioneering woman evangelist.

Harriet Livermore lived a life of extremes. She experienced two decades of fame as one of the most popular, recognized female preachers, was later mocked, and eventually died in obscurity. She had a youth of wealth, privilege, and social status, yet willingly gave it all up to pursue a spiritual life, frequently living in absolute poverty. She came from a family of political leaders, yet advocated for what she believed with no regard for public opinion. She preached with equal fervor to the leaders of the country in the halls of Congress and to society's criminals and victims in asylums and prisons. She preached to laborers on the wharves and to ladies in high society.

Harriet knew the possible price of following her convictions and willingly accepted the hardships and consequences. With uncanny foresight, in 1835 Harriet acknowledged her path: "The cry of 'crazy woman'—'fanatic'—or of 'delusion,' 'enthusiasm and madness,' will not move me, I humbly trust, from my purpose, to blow the trumpet—to sound the alarm—and shout aloud."

HARRIET PATIENCE DAME

1845-1900

Civil War Battle Nurse

SPEAKING QUIET WORDS OF COMFORT, Harriet cleaned and wrapped the soldier's bleeding bayonet wound. She efficiently tied a tourniquet on the next man's leg, mangled by a cannonball. Continuing down the line, she gently closed the eyes of a soldier for whom it was too late. There was no time to spend on the dead; they were moved out and piled in heaps to make room for the endless flow of wounded men. This was not the medicine Harriet practiced as a nurse in Concord, New Hampshire. Where were the bandages, the salves, and the beds? There was no time to wonder, only to learn and to do. Harriet had quickly become immersed in the carnage of the Civil War.

When the Civil War broke out in 1861, President Abraham Lincoln called for volunteers to defend the Union. Men of New Hampshire responded, forming regiments of volunteer infantry. The *New Hampshire Telegraph* asked women to organize evenings of dancing and entertainment to raise money. Saying "an extra blanket, stockings and clothing will save more lives than revolvers," the plea went out to supply the men heading south.

Photo courtesy of Ken Leidner and the New Hampshire Veterans Association

Harriet Patience Dame stands at the Weirs Beach encampment,
proudly wearing her medals as she does in the New Hampshire
State House painting.

Forty-six-year-old Harriet Patience Dame worked as a nurse and was not content to sponsor dances. Born and raised in New Hampshire, she immediately volunteered her Concord home "for hospital purposes." Hoping to help through her nursing skills, she offered to go south with the New Hampshire infantry. There were no standards for protecting women on the battlefront so, like many, New Hampshire's Governor Nathaniel S. Berry objected to women in the field. Harriet's employers also insisted she stay on the job in New Hampshire. Harriet bided her time and hoped for an opportunity to join the men at the front.

The volunteers left in June with only a regimental surgeon for medical staff. Battles and illnesses took their toll on the men and soon the surgeon was desperately in need of help. He requested two nurse "matrons." Harriet quickly applied, was selected, and headed south.

Harriet caught up with the men of New Hampshire's Second Regiment outside Washington just as the first battle at Bull Run began. Before even reaching the surgeon's tent, Harriet treated the first wounded soldier she saw. Then another. Then another. And another. Hour after hour, the battle raged. Harriet was quickly initiated into the horrors of battlefield medicine and met the challenge with skill and compassion.

Unaware of the realities of warfare, excited Washington residents had packed picnic lunches and ridden in carriages to the hillsides outside the city. Watching the battle unfold, the shock of the bloodbath overshadowed their alarm at the Union army's defeat. The wounded soon filled the unprepared capital. Houses, churches, and schools were converted into makeshift hospitals even before the battle outside the city had ended.

Shortly after Bull Run, the other matron requested by the regimental surgeon returned to New England and only Harriet was left. In the midst of battles, Harriet moved from man to man, saving as many as she could, and trying to comfort those she could not. In between she camped and marched with the infantry. Harriet, with her feet encased in heavy rubber boots and a piece of green mosquito netting tied on as her only bonnet, became a familiar presence. As the battle list grew, some stood out in her mind. Harrison's Landing—two weeks without a tent or seeing another woman's face. Fair Oaks—an unexploded shell ripped through her tent. Fredericksburg—Harriet and the men almost froze outside in the December cold. Gettysburg—bodies awaiting burial stacked on wagons. The incessant buzzing of green flies mixed with the sounds of the wounded and dying. Harriet never complained or asked for special accommodation. She hiked up her long skirts and plowed through the grass and mud, scrabbling through underbrush and up rocky hills. They went days with little sleep, alternating pitched battles with tedious marches, which were often just as deadly. Harriet had become much more than a nurse. She felt a true bond with the men fighting around her.

In June 1862 General Joseph Hooker had to order a march back to Virginia. It was 120 miles and most of the sick and wounded could not possibly walk that far. Harriet knew many would be left behind to certain death and so she immediately set to work. First Harriet paired those who could at least stand with those able to walk. They could help each other, shuffling forward, however slow their progress. She organized the cooks to move up and down the lines with cups of steaming coffee. Then, bribing and begging, cajoling and commandeering, she wrangled space for the weakest on wagons and carts. Harriet would do anything in her power to keep the men alive to return to their mothers, wives, children, and loved ones waiting in New Hampshire.

Illness also posed terrible dangers to the troops. Bouts of dysentery and typhoid swept through the camps. To men exhausted and suffering from exposure, the winter brought waves of pneumonia. Soldiers weakened by wounds or infections struggled to survive. Harriet nursed them all, disregarding the personal risk of infection.

When there were large numbers of men too seriously wounded or ill to continue with the regiment, someone needed to stay behind and care for them. Occasionally Harriet was assigned to those field hospitals for temporary duty. The hospitals were often unclean, unsupplied, and understaffed. Frequently food, clothing, and even bandages were dangerously scarce. Serving as matron of the Eighteenth Corps Hospital, Harriet was the only nurse for several months. In between caring for the critically ill men, she spent her precious sitting moments tediously cutting and rolling cloth for bandages. Even her spare time was spent in aid of "her boys."

Despite being far from home, Harriet worked with the New Hampshire Relief Association to help distribute badly needed supplies. In 1862 the State Aid Society at Concord alone reported collecting and sending:

522 quilts, 2003 bedsacks, 1127 sheets, unrecorded number of pillowcases, 1919 cotton and 818 woolen shirts, 882 woolen drawers, 2063 pairs of stockings, 3905 towels and napkins, 4795 handkerchiefs, and 21,768 barrels and jars of miscellaneous contents, besides $3,292.81.

The men of the New Hampshire regiments were her family now, and she took care of them. When money was short, Harriet never hesitated to reach into her meager personal savings to meet the needs of the men. She secured food, supplies, and transportation home for disabled soldiers. Sometimes Harriet even paid for shipping home the bodies of the dead.

Harriet did not limit her attentions to men from New Hampshire. As the months turned into years, she became a familiar figure to men from all areas of the country and both sides of the conflict. She seemed to be everywhere; marching through woods with the men, sleeping curled on the ground, nursing battle wounds in the field through the night, burying the dead, and, no doubt, arguing with anyone who tried to stop her work. She moved to wherever she was needed and, once the need was met, moved on to the next person. An unknown regimental soldier later wrote: "She was everywhere and always on time. She had no special favors to give, but used every sufferer alike. It mattered not whether the soldier was rich or poor." Years later veteran Michael A. Dillon explained how universally Harriet was admired and respected:

> Call the roll of the Second New Hampshire, First, Eleventh, Sixteenth Massachusetts, and Twenty-Sixth Pennsylvania Volunteers, and many regiments of Union and Confederate troops, and ask them, "What of Miss Dame?" and their answer will be "God bless her, she has done for us as our mothers would have done."

Although not a mother herself, Harriet was still a force to be reckoned with. In addition to remarkable courage, she had an iron will. In August 1862, during the Second Battle of Bull Run, Harriet was nursing the wounded at a house in Centreville, Virginia, on the outskirts of the battle. When the army fell back, she and the Army surgeon began transporting the wounded and sick back to Washington. Before going two miles, they were captured by rebel guards. Harriet later wrote about the incident: "We were stopped, but not until I had made the man call the officer of the guard, and I told him they had no right to stop me; their women were never stopped by Unions." She talked her way into getting a tent where she could wait, unintimidated, to confront the commander. A Confederate soldier from Kentucky came to interview her. When he suggested, "You have got too far down in Dixie, haven't you?" she answered boldly, "No, not so far but what I am going farther." She stated that she planned to go to the Confederate capital in Richmond. The soldier explained they weren't sending Union prisoners to Richmond at that point. "I told him that was not what I meant, [I] was going there under the old [Union] flag. He laughed and said I was as spunky as Kentucky women were." When he offered soup made of Yankee beans, she shot back that "a Yankee did not make the soup, sure, or it would have been better." Before long, Harriet was released to walk back to Centreville. Perhaps it is no surprise that Harriet was known by many Confederate units as simply "that Yankee woman."

Harriet was indeed a Yankee, but she didn't ask sides when a wounded soldier needed her help. She nursed the wounded, Union or Confederate, and won the respect of men on both sides of the conflict. Although unconfirmed, there are newspaper reports of another capture that resulted in her release with an apology and praise for her care of wounded Confederate and Union alike. Harriet was known and respected for her nursing, but it is easy to believe part of her reputation and respect was built on that fearless Yankee spunk.

When New Hampshire's Governor Joseph Gilmore needed someone to report to him the conditions of the New Hampshire troops around Charleston, Harriet was sent. Always thorough and blunt, she investigated and sent a frank report detailing the bad shape the troops were in and included detailed recommendations for changes. Harriet was not afraid to confront high officials advocating better conditions for the men in the field, and she embraced every opportunity.

In November 1863 Harriet headed north on the *Argo* as the only medical personnel for the ship loaded with soldiers who were sick, wounded, or heading home. On board, General John T.

Sprague of New York was horrified by the conditions. A small baggage room was used for the most seriously wounded. The *Argo* had been filled with cattle on the trip south. Now the still-filthy hold was the only space left for the rest of the ill and wounded. The few crew cabins were reserved for officers. Offered one, Harriet instead gave hers to a regimental private who was very weak. "How I did long for a big pocket filled with shoulder straps," she later recalled. Using the shoulder-strap insignia to represent wounded enlistees as officers, she could have secured better quarters for them.

Throughout the trip Harriet worked with a chaplain of the Seventh New Hampshire Regiment, scrounging scant supplies from the ship's captain in a desperate attempt to make the men a bit more comfortable. General Sprague asked Harriet to report the conditions to Surgeon-General Joseph Barnes in Washington, and he followed up with a letter of his own. Harriet again had specific ideas and was both clear and vehement in conveying the men's needs to General Barnes. Soon new standards were ordered for boats transporting the wounded. Every such military boat was to be equipped with hospital accommodations, supplies, and at least one surgeon on board.

Harriet continued with the New Hampshire regiments more than four years. They participated in at least twenty major battles and marched more than six thousand miles. Harriet never took a furlough or a sick leave. Even after the South's defeat, she stayed. If the men were still in service, so was she. Finally, on Christmas Day 1865, Harriet shared a wonderful celebration. The Second New Hampshire Regiment was mustered out. Her boys were going home.

After the war Harriet was given a Treasury Department position in Washington, a job she held into her eighties. The war was over but the hundreds of soldiers whose lives she had touched did not forget her. A petition drive began to grant government pensions to nurses who had served at least three months during the Civil War. More than six hundred soldiers and officers signed one of the petitions executed by General Patterson requesting that Harriet Patience Dame be placed on the pension rolls. On June 23, 1884, the Chairman of the Committee on Pensions, Senator Henry Blair, presented bill #3307 to Congress. He read tributes from some of Harriet's former comrades. General Gilman Marston, commander of the Second Regiment, said:

> She sought no soft place, but wherever her regiment went she went, often marching on foot and camping without tent on the field. She was always present when most needed, and to the suffering, whether Yank or Greyback—it made no difference—she was truly an angel of mercy. . . . Miss Dame was the bravest woman I ever knew. I have seen her face a battery without flinching, while a man took refuge behind her to avoid the flying fragments of bursting shells.

Company H's Michael A. Dillon, who had been wounded at the Second Battle of Bull Run and was a Medal of Honor recipient, described Harriet's efforts:

> I can speak of personal knowledge for I have seen her under fire on many a hard fought field, and when lying on my back shot through the body, unable to move a finger, with, as everybody thought, my last breath going out, and with shot and shell raining around us, as if the very heavens were about to fall, she at that time was indeed to me a ministering angel, and I candidly believe if it were not for her I could not have written this letter to-day.

Initially, Harriet had protested the efforts to get her pensioned. Finally she had acquiesced, writing a friend of the regiments' efforts:

". . . they have risen in their wrath and say if I don't keep quiet they will put a real army sticking plaster over my mouth!" Now the men of the Senate listened as Harriet's story was told. Chairman Blair outlined, month by month, the service of Harriet Patience Dame, citing examples of her courage, her skill, and her comfort. It was no surprise when the bill passed.

The next year Dorothea Dix founded the Army Nurses Association, and Harriet was honored to serve as its second national president. While in Washington, Harriet was active in the Episcopal Church and the Cathedral School it sponsored. Never parading her faith, Harriet showed it with her actions. With no children of her own to educate, Harriet endowed a scholarship at the National Cathedral School in Washington, D.C., with the stated purpose "to insure the Christian education of young women."

Although Harriet continued her job in Washington, she kept in close touch with New Hampshire. She continued to maintain a home there and visited often. Given an eight-acre site, New Hampshire veterans groups had begun building headquarters at Lake Winnipesaukee's Weirs Beach. When the state legislature voted that five hundred dollars be given to Harriet for her "extraordinary public service," Harriet used the money for a headquarters building for the Second Regiment. She eventually contributed a thousand dollars to the committee of veterans toward the Victorian-style building that soon overlooked the mountains and lake. Built in 1886, it became the site for annual gatherings of the New Hampshire Veterans Association. Harriet was an honored guest each time. She rarely missed a reunion, and the vets said they couldn't have a good time without her.

When Harriet returned to Concord year-round, she was welcomed and honored. A *New England Magazine* article in June 1895 recognized her accomplishments. Saying Harriet was "perhaps Concord's most valuable contribution to the Civil War" the article described her as "a woman absolutely free from self-seeking, she has earned the gratitude of all who know her, and she cares little for any other reward."

Harriet had earned the gratitude of all who had known her, and the men to whom she had been so devoted now had a chance to express their thanks. At Weirs Beach they set aside a special bedroom just for her. Harriet's rheumatism worsened, eventually requiring crutches. As moving about became painfully difficult, it was the veterans who assisted her, as she had once assisted them. Each morning she pinned on the medals they had given her at the close of that terrible war: The Cross of the 188th Corps. The Diamond from the Third Corps of General Joseph Hooker's division. The Heart of the 128th Corps, in respect of her courage and devotion. The medal inscribed to Harriet P. Dame by the veterans of the Second New Hampshire Regiment. She would join the men to tell stories and reminisce about all those days and nights they had shared. Harriet was content, surrounded by the voices of the old friends she had helped bring home.

In early 1900 Harriet's health deteriorated and, after a fall in her bedroom, she became bedridden. Notes and flowers flooded in as word of her confinement spread. Statewide, officials joined veterans' organizations, passing official resolutions expressing deep sympathy for her poor health and the "hope that she would be spared for many years to come." However, on the evening of April 24, 1900, Harriet Patience Dame passed away.

Within days state newspapers published notices calling "all comrades of the old Second New Hampshire" to show their "love, affection and esteem for the many kindnesses received from this noble woman while on the march, in bivouac, or in camp, by attending the funeral of our dearest comrade, Miss Harriet P. Dame."

They came by the hundreds, turned out in tribute to this unique woman. Harriet had been comrade and nurse, advocate and companion, strength and comfort, not only in battle, but also for a lifetime. Her body lay in state at St. Paul's Church with an honor guard of "her boys" surrounding the bier while hundreds lined up to pay their respects. Newspapers later reported, "as church service began the clouds, which had been rather lowering and sending down occasional drops, broke open and sent down a whole flood of light upon the assembly." After the service whole companies of veterans led the pallbearers' procession to the Blossom Hill Cemetery. Among the many rows of honored dignitaries were state governors and national officers of the Women's Relief Corp, veteran's organizations, and the National Association of War Nurses. A detail from the Second Regiment's Company E fired a salute while a regimental musician played taps. As the first rifle volley was fired, a flock of white doves was released. News reports commented on the doves "circling round and round the spot until the service was over."

Harriet Patience Dame's obituary closed with these words: "Her memory will live so long as self-sacrifice, patriotic devotion, and noble endeavor have power to sway men's emotions." Those words have proven true. The following year the New Hampshire legislature appropriated money for a portrait of Harriet Patience Dame. When the painting was unveiled at the State House in 1901, she was the first woman so honored. A Concord school bears her name, and at Washington's Cathedral School, her scholarship continues to aid young women annually. More than 140 years after she first walked a battlefield, the singular impact of Harriet's work is still recognized and honored today. In 2002 Harriet was voted into the American Nurses Association Hall of Fame. The citation singled out the way Harriet "repeatedly rose to challenges presented to her no matter how monumental" and acknowledged that Harriet's work had resulted in "a dramatic change in the way the military delivered health care."

Her boys would be proud.

MARY BAKER EDDY

1821–1910

Mother of Christian Science

TALKING WITH HER FRIENDS, MARY BAKER discussed the night's agenda. The winter had been difficult in Lynn, Massachusetts, and the women had to tread carefully along icy sidewalks. But February weather wasn't going to stop them from their Friday night temperance meeting. As presiding officer in 1866 of the women's branch of the temperance society, Mary took her responsibilities seriously and had planned the agenda carefully. Suddenly Mary's feet slipped on the ice and she fell to the ground, hitting her head and was knocked unconscious. Mary's friends, unable to rouse her, carried her to a nearby house and called for a doctor.

The doctor who tended Mary through the night had grave concerns. He told the anxious ladies that, if Mary survived, her head injuries were likely to make her a permanent invalid. The next day Mary was moved to her home in Swampscot where the newspapers reported she was awake but still in critical condition. The third day was a Sunday and Mary's pastor called on her in the morning before going to services. Shocked by her weak and failing condition, he promised to come back in the afternoon but was not

Mary Baker Eddy, April 9, 1886, in Boston,
Massachusetts, at the age of sixty-five.

at all sure she would still be alive. Mary asked to be left alone with her Bible to pray.

Born July 16, 1821, Mary Baker was the youngest of six children born on their hillside farm in Bow, New Hampshire, to long-time residents Mark and Abigail Baker. Despite almost constant poor health, Mary had a cheerful disposition, showing particular kindness to small animals. The Baker home was a strongly religious, Congregationalist home. Mark Baker saw God as a stern disciplinarian, whereas Abigail believed in a more joyful, loving God. As a child Mary loved to imitate her mother and grandmother, sitting in a rocker and looking at her Bible. Mary missed most of her early schooling but learned to bake, spin, sew, make soap and candles, and other home skills of farm life.

At twelve, Mary joined the Congregational Church where she remained a member until 1879. With the family, she attended a series of revival meetings at the Methodist and Congregational churches, but never was comfortable with their concepts of predestination or eternal punishment even after repentance.

With a fair complexion, wavy brown hair, and long dark lashes framing her expressive eyes, Mary was considered beautiful by many. At twenty-two she married George Glover, a successful builder active in the Masons, and they moved to Charleston, South Carolina. The following summer George died suddenly, and Mary, six months pregnant, moved back to New Hampshire where, in September, her son George was born. Mary's always-fragile health failed, leaving her unable to care for the baby without help.

The Masons helped the destitute widow by supporting her efforts to open a small private school, much like a kindergarten, but it was unsuccessful. Mary was again dependent on family and friends for her support and for George's care. At one point she was to marry John Bartlett, a local lawyer. In 1849 he joined the many heading to California with the gold rush hoping to check out

California's employment opportunities before returning to marry. By the end of the year Mary received a letter that John had died in Sacramento. Mary's mother had died just weeks before Mary learned of John's death, and the double blow was too much for her. Mary once again became ill and had to ask others to take in George and raise him until she was well.

Three years later, June 21, 1853, Mary married traveling dentist Daniel Patterson, who had promised that George could live with them. But perhaps because of Mary's continued frailty, Daniel changed his mind. Two years later the Pattersons moved to North Groton, New Hampshire, to be closer to the family raising George—but when that family suddenly moved with George to Minnesota, Mary suffered almost complete collapse. Patterson, on the road most of the time, was little help to Mary, who spent months alone with only a blind teenage girl as companion and housekeeper. Mary and Daniel moved frequently, and Daniel, never a faithful husband, abandoned her more and more often.

Mary spent most of the years between 1856 and 1862 in and out of bed. While bedridden she would read her Bible and take note of particularly comforting scriptures she found, often the stories of Jesus healing the sick and infirm. She tried all kinds of homeopathic treatments, even several months in a water-cure facility, to find a way to restore her health.

During those searches Mary learned of Phineas Quimby, a healer from Portland, Maine. She wrote him after receiving one of his flyers, but he was unwilling to come to her. Determined, Mary decided to go to Portland herself. On her first visit she had to be carried into his office because she was so weak. After several weeks of treatment Mary could easily climb to the Portland City Hall dome, more than 170 steps. The cure was remarkable, but temporary, so Mary returned to Portland several times over the next few years trying to learn more and more about Quimby's methods.

Near death after her fall in Lynn and with doctors giving up on her, Mary sought strength from her Bible. She later recounted reading in Mark 3:1–5 the account of Jesus's Sunday healing of a man's withered hand. Deep in prayer, Mary tried to summon the power of that healing for her. Several hours later those sitting vigil outside her door were stunned to see her open the door and walk into the room, seemingly well. When the minister returned he questioned her explanation for the miraculous change. With each doubt Mary seemed to weaken and after he left, she returned to her room and to her Bible. This time the key passage that struck her was Matthew 9:5, and she meditated and prayed on the "Arise and walk" verses. By the next morning Mary's strength had returned, and this time it lasted.

Mary's health may have endured, but her marriage did not. A few months later, Daniel ran off with another woman. Although they were still legally married, Mary and Daniel never lived together again. Despite this emotional trauma, Mary remained healthy and energized in a way she had rarely, if ever, experienced.

Mary spent the next nine years studying the Bible, developing deep belief in a system of prayer-based healing. She lived in several different towns in eastern Massachusetts, boarding with families and occasionally speaking and teaching about her new system of healing. She returned to Lynn in 1870 and began a partnership with a young Richard Kennedy. Together they rented a five-room apartment, which they used as offices and lodging. He hung his shingle as a doctor; she taught and began writing down her thoughts on spirituality and healing. Mary had been ill most of her life and had faced constant financial and emotional hardships. Returning from an 1872 visit to New Hampshire, Mary realized that she finally was healthy, confident, and financially stable. The following year she finally divorced Daniel Patterson on grounds of desertion.

Back in Boston, Mary bought a two-and-a-half-story building at 8 Broad Street and started formal classes. Early students paid one hundred dollars for a set of twelve lessons, later raised to three hundred dollars. As Mary's beliefs evolved they became more distinct from Quimby's, more uniquely her own. Reading her Bible, Mary became inspired by Isaiah 30:8: "Now go, write it before them in a table, and note it in a book, that it may be for the time to come for ever and ever." Despite a complete lack of training, she gathered her notes and began to assemble them into the beginnings of a book to explain her unique beliefs and methods. Mary created a writing sanctuary in a tiny bedroom. Spartan at best, the room contained barely more than a rocker and a simple writing table, lamp, and chair tucked under the steeply sloping eaves above the second floor.

Mary's students were few, but eager, loyal, and supportive. After two rounds of rejections and revisions, she announced the 456-page manuscript's completion. Two students paid in advance for printing a thousand copies. The manuscript was delivered to Boston printer W. F. Brown on September 5, 1874. One 1875 reviewer stated *Science and Health with Key to the Scriptures* "is indeed wholly original, but it will never be read."

As the number of those believing in spiritual healing grew, Mary broke formally with her former Congregational Church back in Tilton, New Hampshire. In July 1876, fifty-five-year-old Mary formed the Christian Science Association to bring together her followers and provide an organization to support their faith, healing, and teaching.

Among the students in the new Christian Science Association was Asa Gilbert Eddy, a sewing machine salesman who believed his heart problems had been healed after studying Christian Science with Mary. On January 1, 1877, a Unitarian minister married Gilbert and Mary Baker.

The next year Mary Baker Eddy accepted a call to preach at the Tabernacle Baptist Church, and her beliefs gained a wider audience. Soon enthusiastic listeners crowded the church for her weekly sermons. One popular and pivotal sermon was "Christian Healing." Mary read biblical accounts of Jesus and his disciples healing the sick. She believed she could use the scriptures to duplicate faith-based cures. Mary expected mainstream churches to accept her healing ministry, but not everyone was supportive. Mary reached a turning point when some ministers publicly denounced her beliefs as blasphemous. Her unique system of prayer and scripture-based healing no longer had a place in traditional religion.

The Christian Science Association voted on April 12, 1879, to establish an independent religion and elect Mary president. Massachusetts granted a charter that August to The First Church of Christ, Scientist and services began. Meeting at first in homes, the services were simple. Silent prayer and The Lord's Prayer were included, but Mary's Bible-based sermons and the time for question and answers about spiritual healing were the focus. Mary wrote in her *Manual of the Mother Church* that the mission was "to commemorate the word and works of our Master [Jesus Christ], which should reinstate primitive Christianity and its lost element of healing."

With interest in her methods of spiritual healing growing, Mary spent the summer of 1880 in Concord, New Hampshire, working on a new revision of *Science and Health* and publishing "Christian Healing" and other popular sermons. Mary also started planning a college to train teachers of Christian Science. On January 31, 1881, the Massachusetts Metaphysical College was chartered with the power to grant degrees, and classes began that summer in Boston. The next spring it opened in a four-story graystone on Columbus Avenue.

Shortly after moving into 560 Columbus Avenue, Gilbert Eddy died, and Mary, now sixty-two and twice widowed, withdrew for more than a month of seclusion in Vermont. When she returned she poured all her energy into Christian Science. She hired Calvin Frye, a former student from Lawrence, Massachusetts, to serve as her secretary and spokesman. He stayed with her for the next twenty-eight years, becoming a confidant and constant support.

The next decade was hectic with the start of the *Journal of Christian Science* (later renamed *The Christian Science Journal*) that assisted the spread of influence beyond New England. Mary also kept an active correspondence with former students now living all across the country. As the movement spread, Mary did not always approve of the way her teachings were presented, and she formed a National Christian Science Association, holding conventions to maintain more control over her message. The sixteenth edition of *Science and Health* was far more coherent and useful, after work by James Wiggin, a highly skilled literary editor. Mary bought a five-story townhouse on Commonwealth Avenue and opened her first Christian Science reading room. She wrote and published pamphlets, articles, and lectures. Christian Science grew to 250 trained practitioners, 90 societies, 20 churches, and 33 academies. Mary traveled to Chicago for a meeting of Christian Scientists and spoke to more than four thousand listeners. She also spoke to huge crowds in New York City. By 1888 Mary's work finally earned her financial stability and comfort in her sixties. At age sixty-seven, she resigned as pastor of the Boston church, closed the college, turned control of the *Journal* to the national association, and moved to Concord, New Hampshire, full time for her first "vacation" in twenty-five years.

After initially living downtown Mary bought a thirty-six-acre farm and house just outside Concord, naming it Pleasant View. Having retired from active teaching, Mary put her energy into building a permanent, self-sustaining organization that did not require her personal participation. She donated land she owned in

Boston's Back Bay for an edifice to be the Mother Church for her followers. Many followers expected her to return and be pastor or to appoint a successor, but as construction began in 1894 Mary instead named the Bible and the teachings of *Science and Health* as joint pastors of Church of Christ, Scientist. She published a *Manual of the Mother Church* to address the details of management and accepted the title of Pastor Emeritus. When the completed church was dedicated in 1895, Mary did not even attend the dedication, remaining in Concord at Pleasant View. Over the next twenty years, she visited the Mother Church only four times.

Far from cut off from her work, she began the Christian Science Publishing Society in 1898 to publish her writings and maintain a forum for disseminating the message to followers, students, and teachers. Mary enjoyed her retreat at Pleasant View from whose rolling hills she could almost see her Bow birthplace. Mary had the farmhouse redone and gradually flower and vegetable gardens, orchards, lush lawns, and even a decorative pond were added to the wooded estate just outside the state capital.

Although Mary rarely left the estate, she did adopt the city of Concord and its people. The local YMCA, New Hampshire Historical Society, and Shaker Village were beneficiaries of her philanthropy. She helped fund local churches, underwriting the building of the First Congregational Church and the steeple bell for the Methodist Church. Mary also provided for less glamorous, more practical needs. She gave more than a thousand pairs of shoes for school children and gave the money needed to pave Concord's Warren and Main Streets for the first time.

Sunday worshippers at the June 28, 1903, communion service at the Mother Church in Boston were thrilled to learn Mary Baker Eddy was inviting them to come and visit her Pleasant View estate the next day. The opportunity to see her in person was so rare that everyone began making travel arrangements for Concord immediately. Special trains were quickly chartered and tickets printed to transport the faithful from Boston. Those who came by carriage had to leave their carriages waiting outside the closed estate gates and walk the remaining distance. The weather Monday was reasonably warm but drizzly as the crowds grew and grew, reaching an estimated ten thousand people by 1:00 p.m. The estate gates opened at 1:30 and, according to newspapers, the rain stopped and sun shone as Mary came out on the balcony. Dressed in a purple wrap, she greeted the crowd. Mary's short curly hair, now gray, was almost covered by her elaborate hat, and her face showed few wrinkles for a woman of eighty-two. After Mary spoke, the crowd seemed disinclined to leave, singing hymns, the doxology, and reciting the Lord's Prayer, Christian Science statements, and scriptures. Eventually they dispersed and the next day the routine at Pleasant View resumed with Mary's Bible reading, correspondence, religious writing, and carriage rides each afternoon.

Mary spent much of 1906 and 1907 embroiled in controversy. She was named in a series of lawsuits alleging she was incompetent to manage her affairs and was being exploited by some of the people who surrounded her. The press was often vicious in their attacks, particularly those newspapers backed by Joseph Pulitzer. Lawyers' visits, psychiatric evaluations, depositions, and accusations no doubt contributed to Mary's feelings of persecution, betrayal, and abandonment.

When the furor quieted and the dust settled, Mary considered herself vindicated but in need of change. She moved to Chesnut Hill, Massachusetts, January 28, 1908, going by train and accompanied by a doctor. New Hampshire certainly would miss Mary. During her years in Concord, Mary Baker Eddy's generosity to the town was remarkable, totaling slightly more than $1.5 million (more than $40 million in today's money). Prior to her departure the Concord town officers passed a resolution of thanks, citing their appreciation of her life, regretting her departure, and hoping she would continue to hold Concord in high regard.

Even with the move, Mary was still affected by the acrimonious atmosphere of the previous few years. Perhaps hoping to set the record straight, Mary finally authorized an official biography. Still bitter over attacks in the press, particularly her experiences with the Pulitzer newspapers during the lawsuits, Mary decided that the news media could not be trusted to treat Christian Science fairly. She wanted a newspaper that would view the world and its events without the prejudice of religious bias. Since no one else seemed to be doing it, she decided she would. So in 1908, eighty-seven-year-old Mary Baker Eddy published the first issue of *The Christian Science Monitor,* stating its mission "to injure no man, but to bless all mankind."

Determined to anticipate questions that might come up after she was gone, Mary also continued to revise and expand the *Manual of the Mother Church,* but her health and stamina were deteriorating. Mary wrote less and slept more. She continued daily carriage rides and spent evenings listening to the Victrola in the parlor or sitting outside after dinner to watch the stars come out. Followers at the Mother Church continued to imagine a strong if aging leader, but those around Mary daily saw an increasingly delicate, elderly woman.

On December 10, 1910, though terribly frail and suffering from a severe cold, Mary still insisted on her daily ride. On returning, however, she needed to be carried upstairs to her room. Later that afternoon, she was too weak to get up. Mary asked for paper and wrote a few words. Two days later, eighty-nine-year-old Mary Baker Eddy died, leaving behind the slip of paper. On it she had written simply, "God is my life."

Mary Baker Eddy lived during an era when women were considered inferior and were often treated as weak or frail. Eddy's impact is remarkable, even a century after her death. She had no literary, medical, or religious training, yet she wrote a book on prayer and faith-based healing that inspired a worldwide religious movement. *Science and Health,* whose early reviewer predicted it would "never be read," has sold more than ten million copies, breaking all publishing records for religious books other than the Bible. Mary Baker Eddy founded a church that now has branches in more than eighty countries. Financially destitute much of her life, she left an estate of $2.5 million to the Christian Science church. Her *Christian Science Monitor* became the root of an international publishing firm and is now published daily in print and on the Internet. Ironically, the *Christian Science Monitor,* begun partly in competition to Joseph Pulitzer's newspapers, has gone on to win seven Pulitzer prizes, named for Joseph Pulitzer.

Three years before her death, *Human Life* magazine described Mary Baker Eddy as "the most famous, most interesting, most powerful woman in America, if not the world." Nearly ninety years later Eddy was elected to the National Women's Hall of Fame for her "indelible mark on society, religion and journalism" and was honored by the United States Congress for her outstanding achievements and contributions. In 1998 this nineteenth-century woman was named by *Religion and Ethics Newsweekly* as one of the "25 most significant religious figures for 20th Century Americans."

The woman who feared she might die young with "no accomplishments worth remembering" need not have worried. While many mainstream churches still question her beliefs, 400,000 people worldwide continue to base their faith and their health on those beliefs. Mary Baker Eddy's accomplishments are indeed worth remembering.

HARRIET E. WILSON

1825-1900

First African-American Novelist

HARRIET E. WILSON LIVED A LIFE of relative obscurity in a world that was all too happy to ignore her existence. Details of events and emotions that shaped her life often must be inferred rather than proven. Newspapers didn't cover the stories of people like Harriet Wilson. Journalists and historians never considered interviewing Harriet for posterity. No one explored her thinking or documented her life for future study. Despite all that, Harriet E. Wilson now stands as a singular example of determination and accomplishment rare for her race, exceptional for her gender, and remarkable for her time.

In 1859 George C. Rand and Avery, a publishing house in Boston, released its newest books. Among them was a novel with the cumbersome title *Our Nig: Or, Sketches from the Life of a Free Black, in a Two-Story White House, North, Showing That Slavery's Shadows Fall Even There*. The Civil War was still two years away, but the divisions of opinion on slavery were widening. Novels describing the life of fugitive slaves or detailing the trauma for slaves living on the fringes of southern plantations were receiving notice,

This bronze statue by Fern Cunningham depicts Harriet, her son, and her book. The statue, erected in 2006 in Milford, New Hampshire, was sponsored by the Harriet Wilson Project (www.harrietwilsonproject.org).

especially in the North. Yet no contemporary reviews of *Our Nig* have been found, no recognition apparent for its author.

Perhaps *Our Nig* hit too close to home to be a best seller. With its heartfelt themes and vivid descriptions of the pain for slaves in the North, *Our Nig* today is considered unique. But at publication *Our Nig* challenged readers' very comfortable beliefs and assumptions. Most abolitionist writing focused on the horrors of Southern slavery. Northern readers were often tempted to believe they led lives morally superior to southern plantation owners. First, they did not see slavery as a Northern problem, although many Northerners did have slaves. Second, they overlooked their own Northern form of slavery that was filled with injustices and abuse to rival Southern-style slavery. Indentured servitude was a common practice in the North. Many confidently considered that system to be vastly different and eminently more just that the South's system of slavery. *Our Nig* challenged that belief.

Our Nig put readers into the life of Frado, a young, free black girl who was "taken in" by a respectable white family in the North. Through her story, readers are shown a picture of life very different from what they were comfortable imagining. Tormented physically and emotionally, Frado dreams of a day when she can escape such cruelty and live in freedom and safety.

Our Nig might have been notable for the story alone, but the most remarkable fact is its author, Harriet E. Wilson. Harriet was a young black woman, born in Hillsborough County, New Hampshire, and eventually living in Boston. Harriet is the first African American, man or woman, known to publish a novel in America. Her literary milestone, *Our Nig,* stands as the first known novel published by a black woman of any country.

Whether readers knew at the time that the author of *Our Nig* was a black woman is unclear. There were few contemporary women novelists. Some wrote traditional sentimental novels.

Louisa May Alcott had begun to publish her work but was not yet well known. A few were using literature to call for cultural change. *Uncle Tom's Cabin,* Harriet Beecher Stowe's literary indictment of slavery, had been released several years earlier. No one, black or white, woman or man, was telling the story of indentured servitude and its abuses. It was not a happy story to tell or to read.

Our Nig tells the painful story of Frado's servitude in a northern white household. Frado is physically and mentally abused from the age of six to eighteen. Presented as fiction, the novel is told mostly from Frado's viewpoint. However, at the close of the book the author speaks in her own voice, asking readers for help. Needing "sufficient money simply to survive," she doesn't ask for outright charity but for support through the purchase of her story. Perhaps it is not surprising that the uncomfortable novel, with its unflinching depiction of life and its pleading author, quickly disappeared.

National attention did not come for almost 125 years, when Henry Louis Gates Jr. found a worn copy of *Our Nig*. After reading it, Gates began to research the roots of the remarkable novel and its unlikely author. He had stumbled upon a book that would rewrite the history of black literature.

Gates and other scholars researching Harriet Wilson's life faced a difficult challenge. Many old documents have been lost or destroyed and, by modern standards, record keeping in the 1800s was sketchy at best. Records of African Americans are even less complete. There simply was no perceived need to document the lives of slaves and indentured servants in a way that allowed a specific individual to be followed. Sometimes marriage intentions were published, births announced, and obituaries noted, but beyond that there is little concrete information. However, as scholars worked to research and authenticate the life of Harriet Wilson, intriguing similarities emerged between Harriet Wilson the author and Frado, the character Harriet created in *Our Nig*.

Gradually a suspicion grew that *Our Nig* was less fictional than originally assumed. Parallels between settings in the book and in Harriet's life were clear. The life of Frado, the main character, appears mirrored in the provable touchstones of Harriet's life. The blurring of fact and fiction, of novel and autobiography, mixed with the culture of the 1800s, means there is no way to confirm whether each trauma experienced by Frado was shared by Harriet. As in scientific research, questions lead to research, research leads to guesses, and guesses rooted in knowledge become hypotheses. Some hypotheses become provable fact. Others remain hypotheses based on fact. All evidence indicates *Our Nig* is autobiographical. If so, *Our Nig* is perhaps the closest we have to a life journal by its author. Using it as a base, researchers found parallels, hints, and sometimes even confirmation of places and events. Moods and feelings can only be assumed based on what Harriet wrote. By mixing what literary researchers have proven and what is told in *Our Nig,* a picture of Harriet Wilson's life emerges.

In Milford, New Hampshire, a baby girl was born March 15, 1825, to an African-American "hooper of barrels" named Joshua Green and an Irish washerwoman named Margaret. The child was given the name Harriet. We have no recorded descriptions of young Harriet. Most likely she was describing herself as she wrote about the fictional Frado.

> Frado, as they called one of Mag's children, was a beautiful mulatto, with long, curly black hair, and handsome, roguish eyes, sparkling with an exuberance of spirit almost beyond restraint.

When Harriet was four, her father died and her mother abandoned her at the farm of the Nehemiah Hayward Jr. family in Milford, New Hampshire. In *Our Nig* Frado describes being abandoned by her mother, Mag, at the home of the fictional Bell-mont family.

> Mag walked onward to the house leading Frado. A knock at
> the door brought Mrs. Bellmont, and Mag asked if she would
> be willing to let that child stop there while she went to the
> Reed's house to wash, and when she came back she would call
> and get her. It seemed a novel request, but she consented. Why
> the impetuous child entered the house, we cannot tell; the door
> closed, and Mag hastily departed. Frado waited for the close of
> day, which was to bring back her mother. Alas! It never came.
> It was the last time she ever saw or heard of her mother.

In the early 1800s it was not unusual for families to take in orphaned or abandoned children. They would be indentured to the family and responsible for domestic work or help with dairy and harvest work on the farm. The Hayward family was not wealthy, but for the times they were comfortable and likely would have welcomed help on the farm and in the house. Researchers consider the Hayward family as the basis of the Bellmonts in *Our Nig*. Nehemiah Hayward's wife, Rebecca Hutchinson Hayward, was a close relative of the Hutchinson Family Singers, well-known abolitionists of the day. Perhaps Harriet's mother thought this would insure a good upbringing for her child. Apparently she was mistaken.

In *Our Nig,* chapter after chapter describes years of Frado's mistreatment as she suffers both mental and physical abuse through the age of eighteen. A niece in the house orders a sick young Frado, "Bring me some wood, you lazy jade, quick." Struggling, Frado moves too slowly. Asked why, Frado replies, "I am coming as quick as I can." The response? " 'Saucy, impudent nigger, you! Is this the way you answer me?' and taking a large carving knife from the table, she hurled it, in her rage, at the defenceless girl."

There is little reason to think Harriet's teen years were better than what she described of Frado's. The census of June 1, 1840, lists fifteen-year-old Harriet, also known as "Hattie Adams," as still residing with the Haywards during the previous year. Some records hint that "Hattie" was often sick and unable to do the work expected of her. In *Our Nig,* Frado was found sitting one day and harshly commanded by the mistress of the house to get back to work.

> "I am sick," replied Frado, rising and walking slowly to her unfinished task, "and cannot stand long, I feel so bad." Angry that [Frado] should venture a reply to her command, Mrs. Bellmont suddenly inflicted a blow which lay the tottering girl prostrate on the floor. Excited by so much indulgence of a dangerous passion, she seemed left to unrestrained malice; and snatching a towel, stuffed the mouth of the sufferer, and beat her cruelly. Frado hoped she would end her misery by whipping her to death.

Frado's misery did not end and neither did Harriet's. Freedom and independence always seemed out of reach. When unable to do more physical work for the Haywards, Harriet learned sewing and mending. Perhaps she hoped to support herself with those skills after she completed her period of indenture. But after Harriet finally left the Haywards, evidence shows she was far from financially independent. Research suggests that Harriet may have either worked as a household servant, moving from family to family, or worked as a seamstress. A federal census supports this, listing Harriet Adams as a twenty-two-year-old black woman living in the Milford household of Samuel Boyles. The Report of the Overseer of the Poor for the town of Milford lists Harriet as a "Pauper not on the Farm" for the year ending February 15, 1850.

Soon after, twenty-six-year-old Harriet met and married a Thomas Wilson, reportedly from Virginia. Her October 6, 1851, wedding is listed in the Reverend E. H. Hidden's April 1852 report of marriages from the previous year. Frado too fell under the spell of a man.

> . . . she saw [Samuel] often, and thought she knew him. . . . He was a fine, straight negro, whose back showed no marks of the lash, erect as if it never crouched beneath a burden.

Harriet's husband, on the other hand, claimed to have lived under the burden of slavery. Thomas Wilson went all over New England giving speeches about his life as an escaped slave. New England abolitionist groups were eager to hear from public speakers who could tell firsthand about the evils of slavery. Unfortunately, Thomas Wilson may have simply seized an opportunity. Despite what he claimed during his speeches, he admitted to Harriet he had never even been to the South, much less been a slave there. The abolitionists were not the only people conned by Thomas Wilson. Soon after their marriage, he abandoned Harriet, who was pregnant and ill. Frado had strikingly similar trials.

> Occasionally he would leave her to "lecture." These tours were prolonged often to weeks. . . . Samuel was kind to her when at home, but made no provision for his absence, which was at last unprecedented. He left her to her fate, embarked at sea with the disclosure that he had never seen the South, and that his illiterate harangues were humbugs for hungry abolitionists. Once more alone!

Abandoned, Harriet went to the Hillsborough County Poor Farm in Goffstown, New Hampshire, where in May or June of

1852 her son George was born. Both Frado's fictional husband Samuel and Harriet's husband Thomas came back to their wives briefly before returning to sea. Eventually both wives learned of their husband's death in distant parts, leaving each alone and with a young son.

Sometime around 1855, Harriet Wilson sent her son George back to the Poor Farm and moved around trying to make a living for herself and for George. He is listed for several years as a pauper in the Milford report of the Overseers of the Poor. In *Our Nig* Frado left her son not in a group home but with an individual before heading out of state to earn a living.

> . . . she left him in charge of a Mrs. Capon, hoping to recruit her
> health, and gain an easier livelihood for herself and child. . . .
> She passed into the various towns of the State she lived in, then
> into Massachusetts.

Harriet eventually settled in Boston, possibly on Webster Avenue. At the close of *Our Nig,* there is an appendix that contains several testimonial letters regarding Harriet and her efforts to raise enough money to return for George. They describe the strangers who took her in and even helped her in business, including a venture selling hair dye. In *Our Nig,* Frado also attempts selling patent hair dye.

> The heart of a stranger was moved with compassion, and
> bestowed a recipe upon her for restoring gray hair to its former
> color. She availed herself of this great help, and has been quite
> successful; but her health is again failing.

Not only do the letters in the appendix hint at Harriet's sales efforts, researchers have been excited to find extant bottles from that era labeled "Mrs. H. E. Wilson's Hair Dressing." If Harriet's life continued to follow *Our Nig,* her fragile physical health again deterred her efforts at self-sufficiency. Like Frado, Harriet began to write.

> . . . she has felt herself obliged to resort to another method of procuring her bread—that of writing an Autobiography. I trust she will find a ready sale for her interesting work; and let all the friends who purchase a volume, remember they are doing good to one of the most worthy, and I had almost said most unfortunate, of the human family.

As Harriet finished the book, friends wrote appeals to be included in the appendix of *Our Nig* extolling readers to purchase copies so that the proceeds would help Harriet and George begin a happier chapter of their life. "Mrs. H. E. Wilson" copyrighted *Our Nig* on August 18, 1859, and a copy was deposited at the Office of the Clerk of the U.S. District Court of Massachusetts. That same year *Our Nig* was printed and released for sale. But whatever hopes Harriet and her supporters had that proceeds might enable a reunion with George were soon dashed. On February 16, 1860, George died of a fever while at the Poor Farm in Milford. He was seven.

The last reference to Harriet in New Hampshire public records appears to be in 1863 when she is once again listed in Milford by the Report of the Overseers of the Poor. Where she went after that is less clear. There are reports of a Harriet Wilson working as a seamstress in Boston. (Likewise, Frado is described as an "expert with the needle [who] soon equaled her instructress.") Harriet also may have set herself up in a more speculative field. *Banner of Light,* a Spiritualist newspaper of the day in Boston, listed a Hattie Wilson in 1867 as trance reader and lecturer. They describe her as an "eloquent and earnest colored trance medium."

A Hattie Wilson is also reported as living in East Cambridge, Massachusetts, in 1867, and on September 29, 1870, a Harriet Wilson married John Gallatin Robinson in Boston. Some researchers believe she went on to share a podium with well-known Spiritualists of the time before she died in 1900 at Quincy Hospital in Quincy, Massachusetts. Lot 13337 in the "old section" of Quincy's Mount Wollaston Cemetery is unremarkable and gives no hint of anyone unique. No newspaper articles will be found detailing burial ceremonies or remembrances. Harriet's story would wait more than 125 years to be explored.

In 1981 Henry Louis Gates Jr. was a young assistant professor of English and Afro-American Literature. Browsing through a Manhattan bookstore, he was intrigued by the worn copy titled *Our Nig*. He purchased it for fifty dollars, and a month passed before he had time to read it, but as he did, Gates suspected he had found a literary landmark. As he delved into the tantalizing puzzle, he began discovering connections between the supposedly fictional Frado and the life of Harriet Wilson. Working like an archeologist at a dig, Gates spent two years uncovering the history of *Our Nig*. In 1983 he laid out his case for *Our Nig* as fictionalized autobiography. Point by point Gates explained his discoveries in the introduction for a republication of *Our Nig*. Soon literary historians were rewriting the records of black literature.

For a time, awareness of Harriet Wilson's accomplishment remained limited mostly to academics. Then in 2003 a diverse group formed the Harriet Wilson Project to raise awareness and to honor her publicly with a fitting memorial. Three years later, on November 4, a bronze statue was unveiled at Bicentennial Park in Milford, New Hampshire. With a keynote speech by actress and civil rights activist Ruby Dee, a moving dedication paid tribute to Harriet Wilson, attended by two hundred listeners. The statue, created by sculptor Fern Cunningham, depicts Harriet and her son.

Chin raised, Harriet holds her open book, pages flipping, in one palm while holding the hand of young George with the other. Acknowledging that, given the cultural attitudes in the nineteenth century, we will never know for certain how many black writers, men and women, were lost to history, Dee challenged the crowd to honor Harriet and to "celebrate that life, that spirit, that resilience that is a legacy to us all."

Researchers continue working to uncover Harriet Wilson's life. They build on tiny bits, like archeologists constructing from scattered fragments. Most of the details of Harriet Wilson's life may be lost to us forever, but the sum of her life is not in details. The passion and perception of Harriet E. Wilson lives through the words she wrote and the story she told. Through the fictionalized Frado, Harriet documented the kind of life overlooked by most. By getting *Our Nig* published, Harriet made it possible for her story to survive and to be shared more than a century later.

As new readers discover Harriet Wilson or find *Our Nig* and enter her world, Wilson's accomplishment will surely become more widely known. But regardless of recognition the accomplishment still stands. Harriet endured an abusive childhood lacking in both education and freedom. Her adulthood was marked by abandonment, poverty, and struggle. Yet, somehow Harriet Wilson managed to learn to read and write. She then put words to paper to document the life and times that surrounded her. Harriet then managed to get her account published, a groundbreaking milestone both for a woman and for an African American. An extraordinary woman, Harriet Wilson earned a unique place in our literary and cultural history.

LAURA BRIDGMAN

1829–1889

Pioneer in Deaf-Blind Education

EMINENT ENGLISH AUTHOR CHARLES DICKENS WATCHED the preteen
girl and her teacher. The girl sat, leaning slightly on a desk that
held her writing book, with her knitting at her side. With careful
deliberation she wrote in her journal. Letter by letter, the neat,
square-style printing filled a page in perfectly straight lines. One
could almost forget how different this child was, but a closer look
disclosed that while one hand held the pencil, the other used a finger to guide the pencil's placement and movement on the paper.
She was dressed in a neat, simply styled frock and her long dark hair
was braided up and around her head, framing a face radiating intelligence and pleasure. But there was the telltale green ribbon tied
over the child's eyelids, and even the doll at her feet had a green
ribbon fastened over its eyes.

Unobserved at first, Dickens watched the silent teacher and
student whose fingers flew in "animated conversation." Suddenly
he was startled by "an uncouth noise which was rather painful to
hear." Instantly the teacher put her fingers to the girl's lips, the
noise stopped, and the two embraced with obvious affection before

Laura Bridgman in her teens in South Boston, ca. 1845. Photographs of
Laura threading a needle with her tongue and of her "square writing" can
be found in the Laura Bridgman photo gallery at the Perkins Museum
web site, www.perkinsmuseum.org/museum/subsection.php?id=130.

getting back to their studies. This was no ordinary classroom. This was the girl Dickens had been so eager to meet, the famous Laura Bridgman, freed from a childhood of frustration and almost total isolation from the world.

Etna, New Hampshire, was a small village near Hanover, and in early 1831 Daniel Bridgman was a farmer and town selectman. He and his wife Harmony were raising three young daughters on their small farm. The youngest, Laura Dewey Bridgman, was prone to convulsions the whole first year, but by the age of two she was walking, talking, and imitating her sisters. Then a scarlet fever epidemic devastated the family. Both older sisters died and Laura was not expected to live. Week after week she clung to life. For seven weeks she could not eat solid food. Her eyes became infected and unable to tolerate anything but a darkened room. Gradually Laura's parents realized that she might live but never fully recover. For a year Laura required support to walk, and she could not sit up all day for almost two years. Laura eventually regained her health, but the bright, engaging toddler was by then five years old, almost completely cut off from the rest of the world by the illness's catastrophic toll on her body's senses. Laura's sight, hearing, taste, smell, and speech had been decimated. Her mind remained intact and curious, but Laura had only the sense of touch to explore and connect with her world.

Laura clung to her mother and used her fingers to explore everyone and everything. She followed her mother for hours at a time, trying to feel what was happening and trying to copy her mother's actions. Slowly Harmony taught Laura some basic tasks. She organized the household so Laura knew exactly where things were kept. She could find the bowls, plates, and silver and became responsible for setting the table. She learned basic cleaning skills by following strict routines, hand-over-hand copying, and daily repetition. Laura learned to mend, sew, and knit. The family developed a system of gestures to identify each family member and basic needs. In time, Laura could occupy herself for short periods of time instead of constantly shadowing her mother.

Harmony could not always be there. There were two new younger brothers, Addison and John, plus the time-consuming work of the farm and livestock. Help came from an unlikely source. Asa Tenney, one of the Bridgmans' neighbors, had no family of his own and, although an almost reclusive loner, was drawn to the small child. Soon he spent hours with Laura, giving her undivided attention and becoming her guide to the outside world.

Every visit was a new adventure, a new lesson for Laura. The pair walked through fields feeling the different textures of leaves, plants, and flowers. With Asa holding her hand, Laura felt safe when startled by gusts of wind, water cascading past her fingers in a rain-swollen spring, or vibrations of thunder felt through the ground. With infinite patience Asa sought out new wonders for her to experience: a smooth egg, the pulse of a baby bird's heartbeat or flapping wings in her hand, a salamander's slippery skin, the chilly roughness of a frog's back. Although Laura could not begin to understand what the things she touched were, she was building a repertoire of sense memories, and her mind's curiosity was fed.

Despite the efforts of Asa and her parents, Laura was increasingly frustrated by a world she could not understand, and she became harder to manage. Her father was the only one with any success disciplining her or stopping her tantrums or screams. Daniel would stamp the floor hard enough for Laura to feel the vibrations, a signal she must stop what she was doing immediately. A pat on the head or shoulder was a sign of approval and reward. Laura did what she could around the house, but was often bored, restless, and confused, with no way to ask questions or get answers.

One spring Daniel hired James Barrett, a nearby Dartmouth College student, to help organize the town records. Barrett was amazed to see what seven-year-old Laura could do despite her disabilities. Hardly a meek child stuck in a chair, she was an intensely curious, sometimes clingy or temperamental child who was obviously capable of learning skills. Returning to Dartmouth, Barrett told his anatomy professor, Dr. Reuben Mussey, about Laura.

Curious, Mussey visited Laura, did some simple tests, and wrote an article about her limitations and her achievements. In June 1837 Samuel Gridley Howe, recently appointed director of what would become Boston's Perkins Institute for the Blind, read the article and was immediately intrigued. Educational and medical experts of that time thought it impossible to teach language to someone without sight or hearing, but Howe was not convinced. If this child was as curious and quick as she sounded, perhaps this was Howe's chance to test the methods he had in mind. If successful, he would be the first. That July, Howe set off for New Hampshire to visit Laura and convince her parents to let him try. Laura's life was about to change forever.

That October, Harmony Bridgman sat eight-year-old Laura beside her in a carriage, transferred to a stagecoach, and after days of travel, arrived in Boston. Harmony brought Laura to Dr. Howe at his school, and when Harmony left, Laura's lifetime at the Perkins Institute began. With no way to explain what was happening, one can only imagine how terrified and alone Laura must have felt. After a few weeks, she realized the people there were kind, and she began to feel comfortable with Dr. Howe and Mrs. Morton, her new teacher. Together they quickly began Laura's lessons.

They started with familiar objects such as a spoon, fork, key, and mug. Labels with raised letters were attached to each object and Laura's fingers were guided over each letter, then around the object. After just three days Laura could search a pile of raised letter labels and pair each with the matching *un*labeled object. Next, labels were cut into separate letters until Laura could unscramble and rearrange the letters into each object's name. Laura learned to use four sets of movable type and a metal frame to arrange letters as they added more and more objects. Two months later she learned a manual alphabet, each letter felt first in metal type, then shaped into Laura's hand until she could feel the way fingers were placed for each letter. Still, for Laura, it was only the rote actions of a game. Finally the day arrived that Laura comprehended the concept of language. Dr. Howe described it:

> . . . now the truth began to flash upon her, her intellect began to work, she perceived that here was a way by which she could herself make up a sign of anything that was in her own mind, and show it to another mind, and at once her countenance lighted up. . . . I could almost fix upon the moment when this truth dawned upon her mind, and spread its light to her countenance.

Once the door to communication opened, Laura flew through it, eager to absorb everything about the world around her. Her teacher was at her side constantly, for Laura was desperate to learn. She quickly mastered the manual alphabet. Her fingers grew facile and, one hand within the curve of another, she learned noun after noun. The left hand explored a hat as the right received its name: h-a-t. Then verbs—hand feeling a door change position: o-p-e-n . . . s-h-u-t. And then adjectives. Within a year Laura was ready to learn to write.

Blind students at the Perkins Institute were taught an intriguing system called "square writing." Paper was folded in half over a metal plate with parallel grooves. The fold held the paper in place and the grooves, felt by fingers, served as line guides for the top and bottom of each letter. First students learned to make a series of vertical and horizontal lines using the grooved guides, then progressed to letters and words. Once students learned the letters in the first cumulative shape group (c, o, a, u) they started words (c-o-c-o-a) and soon added related or similar shape letters (y, g, q, p). Laura was a quick study. Her left forefinger followed her pencil along, covering each letter within a word as it was written. Pencil frozen at the end of the word, her left finger measured off a space along the groove, then she moved the pencil point to that starting position for another word. In an 1840 Institute report, Dr. Howe wrote:

> . . . the most gratifying acquirement Laura [Bridgman] has made and the one which has given her the most delight is the power of writing a legible hand and expressing her thoughts upon paper. She writes with a pencil in a grooved line and makes her letters clear and distinct. She was sadly puzzled at first to know the meaning of the process to which she was subjected, but, when the idea dawned upon her mind that by means of it she could convey intelligence to her mother, her delight was unbounded.

Laura worked hard and soon was able to send a legible letter to her mother, the beginning of a habit of written correspondence that would be a lifetime practice. Barely sixteen months had passed since her arrival at the Institute. The child who had arrived bewildered, angry, and unaware was now a young girl—eager, curious, and clearly intelligent. Laura could connect to the world at last.

Having acquired language and the ability to communicate, Laura began her general education. Geography: Laura began with her home, then the states, capitals, and rivers of New England, steadily working her way around the world. Math: One lesson at a time, she completed Coburn's Mental Arithmetic series. Science. History. Each day was packed with stimulation and intensive instruction. Often, Laura was frustrated by our quixotic language.

She learned about mumps by feeling the swelling on both sides of a classmate's checks, and when Laura got sick and had swelling on only one side, she insisted it was *not* the mumps, she had "the mump." Studying verb tenses, Laura thought it ridiculous just to rearrange the order of letters—such as "eat" to "ate"—but became annoyed when she could not do the same with other verbs. Without the sound of words there were more confusions. If "al-one" meant to be by oneself, then Laura logically described going with another person as to go "al-two."

Hour upon hour Laura's fingers flew, spelling words and thoughts into her teacher's hand almost faster than an eye could follow. When no one was around she could be seen "talking" to herself, each hand spelling to the other as she laughed and teased her imaginary friend.

Monthly "exhibitions" were held at the Institute to raise awareness and funds for the continued education of its students. As the first deaf-blind child known to acquire language, Laura became a prime attraction. People crowded in to watch her write and demonstrate her knowledge in geography and math. Her fame spread. When Charles Dickens planned his trip to America, one person he insisted on meeting was Laura Bridgman. Now, seeing her extensive knowledge, keen curiosity, and lively disposition, Dickens was captivated. Returning to England he devoted a lengthy chapter in his book, *American Notes,* to sharing the inspiring story of Laura's education.

Laura's teachers used more than books to educate her. They seized every opportunity to take her out into the world to touch, ask, and learn. A circus caravan's arrival in town was the opportunity to feel a leopard and explore an elephant. Tusks. Legs. Trunk. Skin. She even got to feed the elephant countless pieces of apple. When Dr. Howe was preparing for a long ocean voyage, Laura visited the steamship in the harbor. Fingers flying one hand within another, teacher and student toured luxurious staterooms, cabins, and the working kitchen. Curious where the cook got milk and flour to make cakes, Laura was taken first to the pantry and then to visit the cow. Finally they walked the entire length of the ship so Laura could grasp its enormous size. Just as Asa Tenney years earlier had taken her to the seashore to experience seaweed and creatures in shells, Laura spent the next decade learning about the world through her fingers.

Laura's formal education ended when she was twenty, but not her life at the Institute. In the summer of 1852 she tried moving back to the farm in Hanover. She was delighted to be with her family, and her mother had learned the finger alphabet, but most of the time Laura was cut off from easy communication. Once again she felt surrounded by a dark and silent world. She slept poorly, soon did not eat well, and by fall was almost bedridden. When notified, Dr. Howe came at once, and seeing Laura's condition, arranged for her return to the Perkins Institute where she gradually recovered.

Laura never did live independently, always feeling most comfortable among her friends and teachers at the Institute. She craved having people to converse with and the bustle of activities. Recognizing this, Dr. Howe and reformer Dorothea Dix successfully established an endowment to provide for Laura's lifetime support at the Institute. Although she no longer took classes and spent much of the day in her private quarters, Laura found ways to connect.

Having become an expert seamstress, Laura made most of her own clothes on a sewing machine and, for fine hand stitching, deftly threaded a needle with her tongue. She sometimes taught sewing to the Perkins' students. She continued to knit and crochet purses, handkerchiefs, and fine lace, and selling samples of her work brought in a bit of extra money.

A prolific letter writer, Laura maintained active correspondence with people throughout the country. Some, such as Dorothea Dix, and Lucretia Garfield, wife of President James Garfield, had first seen Laura at one of the school's exhibitions, and gradually developed a friendship maintained for years through their letters. When visitors came, Laura loved to "talk" with any who could converse with her through use of the finger alphabet, happily gossiping about friends, events, the world—anything.

Laura loved reading books with raised type and spent hours reading her Bible. Her faith was increasingly important to her, and she memorized many favorite scriptures. She often wrote and signed religious maxims to sell or give to those requesting an autograph of the famous Laura Bridgman. "God is love and truth . . . Laura Bridgman," "God is my light. . . . Laura Bridgman." Sometimes she filled hundreds of slips of paper in a single week.

Laura stayed in touch with her family through letters and enjoyed her family's visits to Boston. Each year she went to Hanover for the pleasant summer months. She enjoyed exploring old haunts and catching up with family and friends but was happy returning to Perkins each fall.

On the fiftieth anniversary of Laura's arrival at Perkins, a party was held there in her honor. Dr. Howe had died almost ten years earlier, but his achievement was reflected in the connections Laura had made so far beyond the Institute. So many came—people of Boston familiar with Laura's occasional letters to the Boston papers, past visitors to the monthly exhibitions who had followed Laura for decades, friends with whom Laura had corresponded, former classmates and teachers from the Institute. Laura was surrounded, and for that day, her increasing frailty was forgotten in the joyful festivities.

The following May a very special visitor arrived at Perkins Institute. Two years earlier the parents of an uncontrollable deaf-blind child had been inspired by Dickens's account of Laura's story. Desperate, they wrote the Institute requesting a teacher. A former student who, though much younger, had been close to Laura was hired. She took a doll with clothes Laura had sewn especially for the child. Now that girl's life had been transformed and awakened, just as Laura's had. Helen Keller and her teacher, Annie Sullivan, met with Laura and spent time at the school. They explored the tactile museum's bird and animal specimens, the thirteen-foot relief globe, and extensive library of raised-letter books. And they played. Helen later recalled:

> In the school where Laura Bridgman was taught I was in my own country. . . I joined the little blind children in their work and play, and talked continually. I was delighted to find that nearly all of my new friends could spell with their fingers. Oh what happiness! To talk freely with other children! To feel at home in the great world!

That joy made Laura happy to be at the Institute. Visits to family and friends outside were fine, but the world where Laura truly felt at home was at Perkins, among the children and staff.

Barely a year after that meeting, on May 24, 1889, Laura Bridgman passed away. Newspapers solemnly marked the passing of a woman whose life had made the public reconsider attitudes about limits versus potential. Dignitaries, family, and friends gathered for a Sunday funeral at the Perkins Institute. A more private farewell was held at her burial in Hanover.

As Helen Keller grew and became world-famous, many forgot the earlier woman whose success began it all. Laura was the first deaf-blind person known to have successfully achieved a general education. From her heartbreaking beginnings grew a model that challenged thinking and inspired a new approach to educating the deaf-blind. Today all children are taught math, geography, science, and the arts. Before Laura Bridgman, no one believed such a handicapped child was capable of even acquiring language. After Laura Bridgman, language was only the beginning.

MARILLA M. RICKER

1840-1920

Freethinking Lawyer

I come before you to declare that my sex is entitled to the
inalienable right to life, liberty, and the pursuit of happiness. . . .
I ask the right to pursue happiness by having a voice in that
government to which I am accountable.

MARILLA MARKS RICKER HANDED THE LETTER with those words
to the startled town officer and matter-of-factly asked that her
name be placed on the voting checklist for the coming election.
Addressed to the town selectmen of Dover, New Hampshire, and
dated March 12, 1870, the letter set forth Marilla's case in calm
detail. Three days later she returned to cast her vote and found her
name had not been added to the roster. Displeased but certainly not
surprised, Marilla questioned why she then was still required to pay
taxes on her land. "If taxation without representation was tyranny
before the Revolutionary War, it is tyranny today. I shall protest
against paying taxes so long as I have no voice in making the laws."
Marilla laid down the challenge.

This is one of only two photographs commonly used of
Marilla Ricker as an adult.

Born March 18, 1840, on a New Durham farm, Marilla Marks Young came from an unusual family. Her mother, Hannah, was a devout Free Will Baptist, and her father, Jonathan, was active in the Freethinker movement. Marilla learned to read by the age of four and preferred climbing trees to playing with dolls. She addressed her mother by her first name and, at age ten, after hearing a particularly fiery sermon on hell, announced she would never attend church again. Jonathan taught her to think independently and to be curious, taking her to town meetings and courtrooms, exposing her to philosophy and politics, and encouraging her aspirations. He is reported to have said Marilla "had a mind of her own ever since she had a mind."

Always an insatiable learner, Marilla was not content with the four months per year most local schools offered. When her district was not in session, Marilla walked several miles to study in a district that was. Sixty years later she recalled: "[I] commenced to teach when I was 16. . . . I sat up to the kitchen table and by the light of a whale oil lamp and a tallow candle prepared myself to teach in the District school." Tall and authoritative, Marilla could hold her own against unruly boys, and she soon had a reputation as a disciplinarian and a born teacher—enthusiastic, fair, and challenging. She also challenged the school committees, causing trouble by replacing the traditional daily Bible readings with Emerson and other modern thinkers.

When the Civil War began, Marilla volunteered to serve as a Union Army nurse but, only twenty-one and totally lacking medical experience, she was turned down. Marilla returned to her classroom and supported the troops by using every minute she was not teaching to send patriotic letters, knit stockings, and donate all the money she could spare.

For seven years Marilla taught in the tiny schools of surrounding districts but resigned in 1863 to marry John Ricker, a fifty-six-year-old faithful Congregationalist. They made their home in Dover. Like all women then, Marilla lost the legal right to own property or sign contracts when she married. Financially, socially, and legally the law considered a married woman an appendage of her husband, completely dependent on him. Barely five years later, John Ricker suddenly became ill and died, leaving Marilla grieving, childless, and alone.

John had left Marilla more than financially secure with a fifty-thousand-dollar legacy, which was a fortune at that time. As a widow Marilla regained legal rights, so she could also inherit Ricker's extensive New Hampshire properties. With this rare position of independence and influence, Marilla could pursue whatever goals and causes she chose.

The following year Marilla left New Hampshire to attend the first National Woman's Suffrage Association convention in Washington, D.C. Speakers challenged women to work for change back at home. Inspired, Marilla had an idea, and as soon as she got home she began researching and refining her arguments meticulously. When election time came, Marilla was ready to argue for her right as a Dover resident and taxpayer to cast a vote. Because of her inheritance Marilla had no fear of repercussions for unpopular opinions. She wrote: "I don't care what people think of me. They can disagree with me as much as they like. I am financially independent. They can't hurt me." Thus empowered, Marilla strode into Town Hall, head erect, and presented her case to the surprised Dover selectmen. With that challenge she began a lifetime of advocating change.

Marilla also began a habit of following through. True to her word, the next year she was back at Dover's Ward Three. Perhaps someone thought they could quiet Marilla by fooling her, because some sources indicate her vote was *accepted* but not *counted* in the tally. Marilla was neither fooled nor quieted. Over the following decades she repeatedly appeared at the Dover polls to cast her vote. Each time she was refused. Each time she objected to "taxation without representation," paid her taxes under formal protest, and reiterated her case.

Marilla asserted that no judge in New Hampshire would refuse to sentence a woman of a crime because the statute said "he." She argued, "How could the word 'he' *in*clude women in the laws regarding penalties but *ex*clude women in laws regarding rights and privileges? So long as women are hanged under the laws, they should have a voice in making them."

Although Marilla continued to maintain her property in Dover and to spend summers in New Hampshire, she moved to Washington, D.C. Free from the financial necessity of a job, she began extensive charitable work for the poor and for women in particular. Continuing her childhood habit, Marilla sat in court whenever possible and soon decided to begin a serious study of law. Becoming a lawyer in the 1800s did not require attending a university or law school—not yet widely available—but usually began as an apprenticeship with experienced lawyers.

Marilla began in the D.C. law offices of Albert G. Riddle and Arthur B. Williams. Some sources say she chose law "as a tool to help the weak and unfetter the oppressed." Others claim she wanted to fight against legal injustice and restrictions. But Marilla herself later stated: "I had no idea of practicing, but thought I'd teach German and Law in some private school."

Something changed her mind and, instead of teaching, she began a new career. On May 12, 1882, Marilla Ricker became the first New Hampshire woman admitted to the practice of law. At age forty-two, she took the bar exam in Washington with eighteen men. She received the highest grade of anyone admitted that year.

Marilla's first public courtroom appearance was during the 1883 "Star Route" cases, a series of notorious mail fraud trials. She was Robert Ingersoll's assistant defense counsel, and by the June "not guilty" verdicts, Marilla had earned the respect of the Washington legal community. It was one of the few times Marilla was involved in a high-profile case.

She did not care about high-profile cases or wealthy clients. She did not need their fees and chose instead to help the poor and friendless who needed legal help. It was not the first time she championed the cause of the unfortunate. Prior to her legal career, in 1879 Marilla had advocated a means for state prisoners in New Hampshire to protest unfair conditions. She instigated legislation that allowed inmates to send sealed letters to the governor without fear of interception and reprisals by the wardens.

In Washington, Marilla made weekly Sunday visits to the District's jails. She brought books, writing materials, and other comforts for the prisoners. Dressed for comfort and practicality, Marilla wore dark, simple dresses rather than the large sleeves and voluminous skirts that were popular. The only feminine details were the ever-present touch of white lace at her neck, her soft voice, and her simple gestures as she moved from prisoner to prisoner listening to their stories and offering advice. Once President Chester A. Arthur appointed her a notary public for the District in 1882, Marilla was able to offer more practical assistance to poor prisoners. Other notaries charged fees, but not Marilla.

Already well-known around the jails, Marilla earned the nickname "the prisoner's friend" for her compassion, encouragement, and legal expertise. She took depositions, applied for releases, and wrote briefs supporting pardons, always waiving her fee for those unable to pay. If unable to handle a destitute prisoner's case personally, Marilla hired another lawyer and paid the fees herself. She fought the injustice of Washington, D.C.'s "poor convict's law." Convicted criminals sentenced with only a fine, if unable to pay that fine, could be imprisoned indefinitely. Marilla filed a court challenge and was successful in overturning the laws. Generous and openhearted, she became a champion for the unfortunate.

Within two years Marilla was appointed a U.S. Commissioner and Examiner in Chancery by the judges of the District's Supreme Court. She was the first woman awarded that quasi-judicial post. That same year she took time off to support her law partner's presidential campaign. The all-female D.C. law office of Belva Lockwood, Marilla Ricker, and Lavinia Dundore was known as "the three graces" and now Lockwood was running for president. Marilla headed the New Hampshire electors for the Equal Rights Party, campaigning vigorously for Lockwood. It was the only time she deviated from a lifetime of staunch Republicanism.

Marilla campaigned all over the country for President Benjamin Harrison and President William McKinley. Beneath Marilla's austere facade was a lively sense of humor that she displayed during lecture tours throughout California and that she employed in adding wit to her pointed editorials. She wrote commentaries on tariff issues and letters to dozens of editors about the currency question. Marilla's experience advocating for others helped her when organizing the first Women's Republican Club in Iowa, working in Washington, and stumping in New Hampshire.

Marilla continued to spend her summers in New Hampshire and continued to stir things up. She kept trying to vote in Dover, faithfully protested her taxes, and broke ground for women in 1889 by successfully filing a petition with the New Hampshire Supreme Court to open the New Hampshire bar to women. The unanimous decision reached by the Court allowed women to seek license to practice in New Hampshire. According to state records, Marilla never actually personally sought admission to practice in New Hampshire; she simply opened the doors for women who would follow.

Marilla also benefited from doors other women opened for her. In 1879 her old friend Belva Lockwood had become the first woman certified to bring cases before the United States Supreme Court. In May 1881, on a motion brought by Emma Gillett, the seventh woman admitted, Marilla became the ninth woman certified to bring cases before the high court.

Continuing to build a network, Marilla conducted classes in Washington for the "Wimodaughsis," a ladies club whose name came from the letters of *wife, mother, daughter, sister.* The club sponsored libraries and helped women gain education and later was incorporated into the Young Women's Christian Association. Marilla personally contacted libraries in New Hampshire, offering to donate books on Freethought, and later donated copies of her own writings. The power of women helping women was becoming more organized as women continued to work for the right to vote.

Although the right to vote continued to elude women, the 1896 Republican platform contained a plank that spoke of women's rights and encouraged them to find a "wider sphere of usefulness." Never one to leave the challenge to others, the following year Marilla began a campaign for a post in foreign service. As if there were nothing unusual about a woman applying for an ambassadorship, Marilla wrote President McKinley expressing her interest in the "post of envoy extraordinary and minister plenipotentiary to Colombia." Marilla did not point out that she was the first woman to seek a foreign ambassadorship or that nothing in the statutes specifically ruled out appointing a woman to that post. Choosing to ignore gender, Marilla based her application on skills and experience only.

Marilla had traveled in Europe extensively over the years, had become fluent in German, Italian, and French, and was eager to learn Spanish. As a respected, experienced lawyer, she had the necessary legal background. Women's suffrage clubs across the country quickly backed her appointment, but Marilla's skills earned much wider support. Both New Hampshire senators and many prominent

Republicans endorsed her. The *Boston Post* wrote an article summarizing Marilla's career and detailing her qualifications for the post. Evaluating her credentials, even the *New York Times* took the position that "except for the extreme novelty of the idea it would be hard to find insuperable objections to the appointment."

McKinley ignored the recommendations and endorsements. Ironically, the letter turning her down arrived addressed to "Marilla M Ricker, Esquire" and began "Dear Sir." There was no reason ever documented and no outraged public outcry when McKinley failed to appoint Marilla, although one report commented that "in doing so [McKinley] passed over a person of remarkable ability and singular achievement."

As with all obstacles Marilla faced, she did not become angry or bitter. She believed rejection was part of the process and accepted defeat philosophically rather than considering it a personal failure. The *Boston Sunday Herald* wrote a lengthy feature on her mix of calm persistence and passionate advocacy:

> Apparently bold and always progressive, she is in reality very timid and always addresses the court with much shyness and trepidation . . . unless she enlists to fight for a principle, then she is loyalty itself, and unflinching.

An editor trying to capture Marilla's spirit for a book on New Hampshire notables summarized: "She is frank, generous, and open hearted, a friend of the unfortunate, a champion of reform causes, a hater of sham and hypocrisy."

Marilla had always considered New Hampshire home, even while working in Washington. In fact, when once introduced as from D.C. she quickly corrected, "No siree, I am a New Hampshire woman! I'm Marilla Ricker from [New] Durham." Gradually she spent more and more of her time back in New Hampshire.

Marilla's political activism did not slow with her return to New Hampshire. She wrote numerous articles on politics and Freethought, was a life member of the Woman Suffrage Association, and served as vice-president at large of the New Hampshire Woman Suffrage Association. Anyone who mistakenly thought Marilla's views might mellow with age needed only to read her latest editorial or hear her rail against "progressives" in the Republican Party.

Marilla's efforts for women's rights and the Republican Party converged in one more political first. Still astute and amazingly vigorous at age seventy, Marilla attempted to run for governor of New Hampshire. When no "regular or stalwart element of the Republican Party applied, and it appeared likely a "progressive" would have the party nomination, Marilla stepped forward.

The primary was to be held September 6, 1910, and on July 9 Marilla paid the required one-hundred-dollar application fee and filed the papers officially declaring herself a candidate. No woman had ever filed for the office of governor, and the secretary of state quickly forwarded Marilla's declaration to the attorney general for instructions.

The only requirements for governor were to be over thirty and a New Hampshire resident for seven years. Marilla pointed out she exceeded both. While the New Hampshire attorney general decided whether "Marilla M. Ricker" could appear on the ballot, she began her campaign. Marilla announced that "justice and equality for all men and women in New Hampshire" would be her rallying cry but not her only agenda. Current issues included tariffs, fortification of the Panama Canal, disposition of the Phillipines, the size of the navy, and the role of the Boston and Maine Railroad in the government economy. Marilla stated clear positions on each, and the media took notice. The *Concord Evening Monitor:* "At every stage of her illustrious and eventful career, she has been a determined and intrepid fighter along all possible pathways of upward progress." The *Portsmouth Times:* "We believe that Mrs. Ricker could fill the governor's chair with credit to herself and honor to the Granite State. And whatever the 'M' stands for, it doesn't stand for 'Mud.' Marilla is no joke!"

On July 30, the ruling came: "The office of governor of this state is a public office and under existing laws women are disqualified to take an official part in the government of this state." The attorney general continued that if a person could not legally hold the office, that person's name could not appear on the ballot. Marilla remained calm but determined, first with court appeals to overturn the ruling, then to the public to enter her name by petition. Newspapers reported that Marilla's attempt to run was attracting "almost world-wide attention, not only with lawyers, but with the public generally."

When trying to run for governor, Marilla explained her platform of "equal rights for all and special privileges for none." On women: "I advocate equal pay for equal work, and no woman can afford to be indifferent to anything that degrades women." On taxation: "The steeple is no more to be excluded from taxation than a smokestack." Her positions on religion prevented her from general acceptance then and still.

The September primary came and went without Marilla's name on the ballot, and so she had no chance. She divided time between her Dover home and the Parker House, a hotel in Boston. For the next few years, she devoted her efforts to writing and publishing books and articles, including regular columns in *The Truth Seeker,* a popular Freethought periodical. Although she continued to do political writing, most was in defense of Freethought ideals. Her writing challenged religion, its institutions, its clergy, and the Bible. In quick succession Marilla published *Four Gospels* (1911), *I Don't Know, Do You?* (1916), and *I Am Not Afraid, Are You?* (1917).

At seventy-eight Marilla wrote a lengthy response to a government survey about the lives of women with unusual occupations. She noted the luxury of choice her inheritance had allowed: "I was financially independent and I amused myself." How fortunate the women's movement was that a woman of Marilla's mind and skills choose to "amuse herself" as she did. Acknowledging controversial positions, Marilla continued, "I am an out-and-out Freethinker and have lectured politically and written much Freethought literature. I'll send you what I consider my best book, *The Four Gospels.*" Her firm, graceful longhand showed no sign of age or frailty, but her closing showed a sense of humility and humor. Mentioning her time in Germany, France, Italy, California, and the Hawaiian Islands, she closed with, "I certainly have had a good time. I feel competent to write the life of a student and a tramp!"

Within the year, Marilla's health began to deteriorate. The Nineteenth Amendment, giving women the right to vote, was formally proposed June 4, 1919, and ratified in just 441 days with Tennessee's August 18, 1920, vote. Some theorize Marilla finally got to vote in Dover, but it seems unlikely. She had spent the last two years in the Dover home of *Dover Tribune* editor John Hogan, living under his conservatorship due to her failing health. But Marilla did not need to actually cast her vote to succeed. For her, opening the doors was enough. She intimated as much during her gubernatorial campaign.

> I'm running for Governor in order to get people into the habit
> of thinking of women as Governors. . . . People have to think
> about a thing for several centuries before they can get acclimated
> to the idea. I want to start the ball a-rolling.

Marilla got a lot of ideas "a-rolling." She believed in freethinking, Republicanism, and women's suffrage. Freethinkers defined

themselves as those "who form opinions without regard for author-
ity or tradition." Marilla not only formed opinions, she announced
them clearly and often. On guilt and innocence, for instance, she
famously stated: "We're all guilty for we have thought the same.
This person possibly was rash enough to do it. Had we been born
under the same circumstances and lived in the same environment
we might have done the same." Marilla's statements on equal
rights, equal pay, and religious tax exemptions are still controversial
almost a century later.

Marilla spent a lifetime trying to break new ground, open
minds, build fellowship, and support fairness and opportunities for
people unlikely to receive either. Her early work protecting New
Hampshire prisoners is echoed in today's laws to protect whistle-
blowers. The New Hampshire Women's Bar Association honors
her work annually. The Marilla M. Ricker Achievement Award is
given "to women lawyers who have achieved professional excel-
lence, or paved the way to success for other women lawyers, or
advanced opportunities for women in the legal profession, or performed exemplary public service on behalf of women."

Almost ninety years after Marilla Ricker's attempt to run for governor was disallowed, a special bill was passed by the New Hampshire
House and Senate. "Marilla Ricker, with vision and the courage to
persevere in the face of enormous odds, unjust law, and unpopular
public opinion, lived a life that changed the course of history of New
Hampshire for the benefit of all people." Opening with those words,
the bill called for a portrait of Marilla to be obtained and displayed in
a place of honor in the Statehouse. At the June 1997 signing, the governor emphasized, "Marilla Ricker is not just notable for what she has
done for women, but for her courage to stand up for what she believed
in." The governor understood very personally what Marilla Ricker did
to pave the way for women. The governor was Jeanne Shaheen, New
Hampshire's first elected female governor.

Marilla still pays a price for her unpopular views. The authorized painting does not hang with honor in the State House. It has never even been painted. The necessary funds were never authorized or raised. Meanwhile, a painting of Governor Shaheen is almost complete and will soon hang in the State House. Doubtless Marilla would have accepted the snub matter-of-factly. Marilla did not expect recognition or require honors. Confident and willing to stand her ground, she was satisfied opening the doors for others. Portrait or not, Marilla Ricker had started "the ball a-rolling."

MARIAN MACDOWELL

1857-1956

Founder of the MacDowell Colony

WHEN TWENTY-THREE-YEAR-OLD MARIAN NEVINS boarded ship for
Germany in the summer of 1880, she envisioned a career in the
arts, but as performer not patron. Marian's father, David, was a
successful New York banker-broker. But he struggled to raise his
five children after their mother Cornelia's death during childbirth
in 1866. Marian, the middle child, was the oldest girl, and she tried
to help her father with the household, particularly her younger
sisters, but he couldn't manage. Soon David sent ten-year-old Marian and her four siblings to live seventy miles away in Connecticut
with two aunts, Lucretia and Caroline Perkins. They had founded a
school the children could attend and were financially able to manage the extra responsibility.

Marian discovered her Aunt Caroline's piano and took to it
immediately. Caroline taught her for four years, by which time
Marian's blossoming talent required more advanced teachers. Recognizing Marian had the potential to become a leading concert
pianist, her teachers challenged her, and soon she spent hours a day
at her beloved piano.

This photograph of Marian MacDowell was taken at the MacDowell Colony's celebration of Marian's ninety-fifth birthday.

Based on the belief that the finest musicians and teachers were in Europe, serious American musicians spent years studying and earning recognition abroad. Fortunately for Marian, her aunts were eager to make that possible for her. They arranged for her to complete her training with the great concert-pianist Clara Schumann, the wife of famed composer Robert Schumann. The plan was that Marian would gain experience performing with the orchestras of Europe under Clara's guidance and then return to the United States and continue a concert career.

When Marian arrived in Germany, Clara Schumann had fallen ill and instead Marian was to study with American composer-pianist Edward MacDowell. MacDowell had been studying in Europe since the age of thirteen and was a highly respected teacher at the Darmstadt Conservatory. Marian studied with Edward for the next four years, and the two grew close. Marion urged Edward to spend more time composing, using the inheritance from her mother to augment his teaching income. Initially reluctant to use Marian's inheritance, he finally acquiesced. The two returned to the United States for two wedding ceremonies—a simple one in New York on July 9, 1884, and a second one July 21 in the Waterford, Connecticut, home where Marian had lived as a child.

Shortly after marrying, the MacDowells returned to Germany and lived frugally to conserve Marian's inheritance. Edward gave recitals that added to this income but would withdraw to compose whenever possible. Marian arranged her life to make conditions the best possible for Edward to perform and compose. She warded off all distractions, even leaving their apartment for hours so Edward could have complete quiet.

Marian's strategy worked. Edward began performing his own compositions throughout Germany. Soon he and his music were in popular demand. He published piano suites and orchestral tone poems that were praised by European conductors and critics.

In 1886 Marian and Edward were eagerly awaiting their first child, but the baby was stillborn. Serious medical complications ended their hopes for children.

However, by 1888 Edward had met Europe's test and became the first American symphonic composer to gain international respect. The MacDowells returned to the United States that autumn to build a career at home.

Settling in Boston, Marian continued her routine. She traveled with Edward during recital trips, managing travel arrangements, packing and laying out his clothes, and standing backstage. In Boston she managed the household, transcribed his music, and served as first audience and critic for each new work. Edward was hired to teach at Columbia University, and the couple moved to New York. As always, Marian tried to maintain a quiet home conducive to inspiration, which was even more difficult in the busyness and noise of Manhattan.

When a concert tour took the MacDowells through New Hampshire, its unblemished nature delighted them both. Marian returned in 1895 and found an abandoned farm in Peterborough. Its acres of quiet woods and fields captivated her, and she immediately wired Edward suggesting they purchase it. As a summer home, she suggested it might be the perfect respite from city life, offering inspiration, solitude, and quiet. Not convinced, he telegraphed back: "All right, in your name, your responsibility." Undaunted Marian acted, paying the $1,500 herself. Marian became the owner of seventy-five acres with a house and wobbly barn. She named the property Hillcrest.

Every summer thereafter the MacDowells exchanged New York's chaos for Peterborough's calm. Marian later wrote that Edward "learned to love and know this little New England town, haunting its hilltops." The "old world atmosphere and spirit of unruffled repose" filled them with nature's peace and inspiration.

Despite the quiet of their Peterborough farm, Marian still often left the house and walked for hours while Edward composed. Roaming the property's wooded hills, she decided to have a hillside studio built as his birthday surprise. The small log cabin with its view of Mount Monadnock was completed in 1899. Edward loved it, often working there all day. Marian packed him picnic lunches and left the wicker basket quietly on his studio porch each noon. Marian and nature had created an idyllic setting for unfettered creativity.

The following years were marked by professional turmoil, debilitating injuries, and illness. Marian had serious abdominal surgery and a long, difficult recovery. Edward left Columbia University in a heated dispute. Soon afterward he was hit by a Hansom cab in New York and within two years was deep in a devastating mental decline. As word of Edward's incurable condition spread, the musical world rallied to raise funds for his care. Marian and Edward had occasionally spoken of the artistic sanctuary Marian had created on their Peterborough property. Philip Hale later described Peterborough's artistic connection:

> [Edward] was on unusually intimate terms with Nature. . . . To him there was strange music in a New Hampshire hillside, in an abandoned farm, in the peculiar bleakness of a landscape, in the suggestion of a spring that is a season in other lands.

Marian began to dream of a colony of artists at Hillcrest. What Edward had found through her picnic lunches and isolated log-cabin studio could inspire other artists. She could free them of daily responsibilities by cooking and cleaning—and surround them with nature by building more scattered studios.

Marian began realizing this dream as Edward's health declined. In 1907 she incorporated an Edward MacDowell Memorial

Association, formed a board, and officially began The MacDowell Colony on the Hillcrest property in Peterborough. The first residents—ever after called "colonists"—were sculptor Helen Farnsworth Mears and her sister, writer Mary Mears. The same summer Arthur Hartman arranged one of Edward's pieces and assigned all its royalties to Edward's care. Marian wrote to him:

> It would be difficult for me to express my appreciation of your truly lovely interest, which has not taken the form of words but has been so active. I hear from all sides how beautifully you have played the little "Wild Rose," and I know the royalties will prove that, in a practical way. How I wish my husband could have heard you play it. He is much the same, a little more helpless, a little nearer the end.

On January 23, 1908, Edward died and was buried at Hillcrest. Nearly $30,000 raised for his care was given to Marian, and she immediately donated it to the new association. Serving as the new enterprise's executive director, Marian gathered the board of directors and threw herself into planning and organizing the budding colony. At age fifty Marian was embarking on a staggering challenge.

The first step was raising funds. Marian brushed up her piano skills and planned a return to the performing career set aside decades before. By 1910 she began giving fund-raising concerts and recitals. After an April 1916 performance in Tennessee, the *Chattanooga* extolled:

> Mrs. Edward MacDowell is one of the most highly gifted pianists who has appeared before a Chattanooga audience in a long time, to say nothing of the program and its construction, which is probably without parallel by way of its uniqueness and artistic scope.

Midway in the program Marian would stand by the piano and tell her audience about the fledgling colony whose grounds had inspired so many of the MacDowell pieces she now played. The *Atlanta Journal* responded to her Georgia concert:

> There were no tricks in her playing. Her technique is clear, scintillating, and full of feeling. Mrs. MacDowell played as she talked—to the point, honest, and always convincing . . . a really great pianist.

Marian appeared anywhere she might raise funds and awareness. Sometimes the priority was the talk and the music a bonus. The minutes of an Illinois MacDowell Club reported:

> Mrs. MacDowell, fortunately for us, was also able to be here, and gave us another of her most entertaining and enlightening talks, following it, by request, with a few selections from her husband's works, played as only she is capable.

Whenever she appeared, listeners left embracing Marion's dream—a place where the creative flow of emerging artists was freed from burdens, intrusions, and responsibilities of daily life.

In a fifteen-year span, Marian appeared in more than six hundred cities, in every state but four, to more than 100,000 people, traveling nearly 200,000 miles and making several coast to coast tours, all at an age when most would slow down. After each tour, Marian gave the board of directors the money raised. Bit by bit the Colony grew, and word spread of this unique place. Marian had more cabins built as more colonists asked to come. She selected each colonist personally. Maintaining the experience was "more valuable for the emerging artist than an established artist," she required signs of talent more than of success. Some came for two weeks, some for two months. The Colony hosted poets, novelists, artists, composers, and sculptors, and the row of wicker baskets to be filled and delivered each noontime grew. Soon the Colony had far more applicants than openings.

When the Tenney Farm adjoining her property became available, Marian jumped at the opportunity to expand the Colony. She went immediately to the village, borrowed the $500 down payment and signed the papers. Only then did she go to the board. She later admitted, "I was terribly excited and happy, and a little scared at what I had done without authority from the directors." As usual, no one could dissuade Marian from her vision. The Tenney purchase added 184 acres, including a farmhouse later converted to a men's dormitory.

In 1925 the country at large began to be aware of the amazing work Marian was enabling at her remarkable colony. The *Pictorial Review* gave its annual $5,000 prize to "the American woman who makes the most valuable contribution to American life during the year" to Marian MacDowell. True to habit, Marian turned the money over to the board of directors.

A significant body of work had been produced now by Colony artists, and Marian added readings of their work during intermissions at her piano concerts. Working her way outward from Peterborough, she performed in tiny village churches and large city auditoriums. By 1928 Marian's concerts and talks had paid off the mortgage. More important, she had built awareness, pride, and a sense of ownership throughout New Hampshire for her beloved MacDowell Colony.

Despite the 1929 stock market crash, Marian was determined the Colony would survive and grow. To extend its season, Marian added central heating to the lodge. She also continued adding studios. Heading back on tour, seventy-three-year-old Marian gave fund-raising concerts through the United States and Canada. She inspired sororities, music clubs, and individuals to pledge funds to sponsor a studio's construction or upkeep.

Marian's single-minded attention enabled the Colony to thrive. Her work was recognized with two honorary degrees—from the New Jersey College for Women and from the University of New Hampshire. Her Colony also was celebrated on its twenty-fifth anniversary by concerts at Carnegie Hall and around the country. In *Musical Quarterly,* composer Amy Beach tried to explain the Colony experience: "It is not merely the absence of noise or other distracting influences. It is the actual communication . . . which can only reach us through the innermost silence."

For her eightieth birthday Marian presented a special fund-raising concert, playing her husband's Second Piano Concerto with the New York Philharmonic. She later boasted, "And I didn't play any wrong notes." After a pause, she grinned and added, "But I did leave some of them out!"

With the Colony popular and respected, Marian could relax a little. But September 21, 1938, everything changed. Nature, the inspiration for so many at the Colony, unleashed a hurricane and devastated the grounds. When the storm cleared, damaged buildings still stood, but not so thousands of tall white pines that had filled 250 acres of the Colony's woods. They lay flattened, scattered in "disorderly piles on the ground," obliterating any semblance of peaceful haven. Composer Aaron Copland, who was there, recalled:

> What one day had been a lovely pine woods now looked like the most desolate war-torn swamp. The road that had taken 10 minutes for me to walk [the day before] took ten men with axes two and a half hours to hack their way through.

Marian wasted no time. The next day she literally bought a local sawmill and, using Colony employees, local men, and Maine loggers, immediately began cutting the downed trees and selling the cordwood. When the board complained she had not been empowered to buy a sawmill, Marian replied, "No, by the time I had permission someone else would have had the sawmill." Marian was nearly as unstoppable a force as the hurricane, and her dream would *not* be ended by a storm.

The money to restore the Colony had to be raised. So, physically frail but mentally as strong and determined as ever, eighty-one-year-old Marian went back on the road for more concerts and more lectures. She also wrote appeals to every woman's club, arts organization, former colonist, and patron she knew. By the summer of 1940, Marian had been given another doctorate (from Middlebury College) and received the Pettee Medal (from the University of New Hampshire). But her greatest joy was reopening eighteen studios to host fifty-three colonists for the first time since the hurricane. Her colony was back.

Maintaining the Colony after America entered World War II was difficult. After the attack on Pearl Harbor, a flurry of letters outlines preparations for possible wartime shortages. Other letters detail arrangements to cover for men going into the Army, as well as the importance of the arts even in wartime.

Around this time Marian developed a cagey new ploy when disagreeing with the board: "This may be my last request. . . . I'm in my 80s and probably won't be at your next meeting." That usually ended debate.

Now living in California for her health, she returned each summer to ensure everything met her standards. Artists' studios had northern light, musicians had grand pianos, and writers had chair heights to their exact needs. Cabins were unobtrusively cleaned while colonists ate a communal breakfast, which even offered a "grump table" to accommodate those who didn't enjoy early morning conversation. The trademark wicker baskets still silently arrived on the porch or doorstep each noon. And each Sunday evening Marian invited colonists to join her for dinner at Hillcrest.

Eventually time and health did catch up with Marian. On November 22, 1946, Marian marked her eighty-ninth birthday and sent the board a telegram.

> Our work has suffered wars, depressions, hurricanes, and floods and has endured. From its successes and failures have come long friendships and precious memories. The MacDowell Colony will not fail of its purpose. Others will carry the burden of the work now firmly established through your efforts and mine. I shall enjoy my remaining years free from managerial responsibility and be proud and happy in the continuing growth and usefulness of our mutual accomplishments.

The board accepted Marian's resignation and granted her two new titles, honorary president of the association and founder of the Colony. She continued as "corresponding secretary."

August 15, 1952, was officially declared "Marian MacDowell Day" statewide, and more than six hundred people gathered on Hillcrest's lawn. Peterborough neighbors mingled with a former New Hampshire governor, two U.S. senators, and an American *Who's Who* of creative artists from every discipline, all there to celebrate Marian's upcoming ninety-fifth birthday. Symbolizing hundreds of former colonists, Thornton Wilder read from his Pulitzer-winning play *Our Town*. The play reflected its Peterborough inspiration and was largely written at the MacDowell Colony. After speeches a leather-bound book of greetings from hundreds of former Colony residents plus representatives of arts organizations throughout the United States and abroad was presented. When all was done, Marian rose to thank those assembled. Surprising everyone, Marian spoke for twenty minutes without notes. Vivid memories and lively anecdotes mingled as she recounted the Colony's evolution from first dream to current reality. Newsmen reported that when Marian closed and took her seat, the crowd was "overcome with emotion" and spontaneously broke into "Auld Lang Syne."

The Town Selectmen of Peterborough arranged to have a cake delivered to Marian in California on her ninety-sixth birthday. The card read: "To Marian MacDowell, Peterborough's First Citizen, Beloved by All New Hampshire." The next February she reluctantly wrote:

> I hate to think I shall never go back to Peterborough, but last summer was too great a strain with the excitement and the journey, and in my 97th year I begin very steadily to lose ground. . . .
> So now I've given Hillcrest back to the Association.

Marian could no longer manage cross-country trips to Hillcrest, but the Colony still received her first thoughts and energy. Though practically blind from cataracts, Marian routinely spent several hours a day dictating or typing letters to former and prospective Colony artists and donors. She averaged nearly a thousand letters a year.

Just three months shy of her ninety-ninth birthday, Marian MacDowell died in Los Angeles, late on August 23, 1956. For days afterward people around the country continued to receive her letters. Working until the end, Marian had written and mailed them the morning of her death. After a Los Angeles funeral, Marian was returned to Peterborough. A mix of neighbors and artists came to honor and praise Marian as she was buried alongside her husband in the small plot on MacDowell Colony grounds. Accolades for her unique contributions filled obituary tributes across the country and around the world. So many obituaries referred to Marian as "Edward MacDowell's wife" that an offended columnist in Illinois pointed out what the artistic community had long known: "So far as influence in the arts is concerned, Edward MacDowell might well be identified as the husband of Marian MacDowell."

In the years since Marian MacDowell's death, her dream has flourished. In the 1960s the MacDowell Colony was designated a Registered National Historic Landmark. As focus on the arts increased during the 1970s and 1980s, the world tallied the growing accomplishments of MacDowell colonists. In a September 29, 1997, White House ceremony, President Bill Clinton awarded the MacDowell Colony the prestigious National Medal of Arts.

Aaron Copland said, "Long before people began talking about culture and the cultural explosion, Mrs. Edward MacDowell in her quiet, but very energetic way *did* something about it. She created this place where culture starts; because it starts in the mind of the artist."

The MacDowell Colony now operates year-round. Its thirty-two studios are still without telephones, still invisible one from another. Artists still have their days free from visitors, work responsibilities, and concerns for food or household, enjoying unfettered creative pursuit. Privacy and isolation are still the rule. Only once each year does the MacDowell Colony open its doors. For one afternoon the public can explore the grounds and studios that host artistic genius.

At age fifty Marian MacDowell chose to focus her experience, energy, and indomitable spirit into developing and pioneering an almost perfect environment for stimulating and supporting creative minds. The MacDowell Colony is no longer a utopian experiment but a proven model that has borne a rich variety of artistic fruit. Describing her work Marian explained, "It's what I've dedicated my life to prevent . . . the *non*writing of the great poem." Not only has the MacDowell Colony served poets but also filmmakers, artists, composers, architects, sculptors, playwrights, and interdisciplinary artists. Colonists have earned a long, dazzling list of Pulitzers, Prix de Romes, Oscars, Grammys, Tony Awards, Guggenheim Fellowships, and prizes in every conceivable field of artistic creation.

A bit embarrassed by the hoopla for her ninety-fifth birthday, Marian told a *Peterborough Transcript* reporter, "I am a very ordinary woman who had an opportunity—and I seized it." Marian created a legacy that passes on opportunities for others to seize. In its first one hundred years, the MacDowell Colony has been a creative fountain of, and for, more than six thousand colonists from forty-nine states and fifty countries. Marian had the talent to pursue her original career as concert pianist, but, instead, she devoted a lifetime nurturing the creative genius of others.

Douglas Moore of Columbia University attempted to summarize the value of this anything but "ordinary woman" when the MacDowell Colony was nearly fifty years old—and fifty years later his prophecy is still on track. Moore said to Marian MacDowell: "There will be millions to come who will salute you and remember you as the most devoted, the most generous, and the most understanding friend that the American artist has ever had."

AMY CHENEY BEACH

1867-1944

Internationally Respected Composer

AMY WATCHED THE RAINDROPS MAKING CROOKED PATHS down the windowpane. Drop after drop, connecting and dividing, richocheting zigzags, drop after drop. Most small children might be fascinated, until almost hypnotized by the random tracings. But Amy was not like most children. She became filled with an overwhelming sadness as she watched each drop fall. Finally she could bear it no more and begged her mother, "Wipe away the tears!"

Amy Marcy Cheney was born September 5, 1867, in Henniker, New Hampshire, and quickly showed unusual musical abilities. At a year old, Amy would sing tunes perfectly after a single hearing. Amy's mother wrote her sister, saying, "Before two years of age she would, when being rocked to sleep in my arms, improvise a perfectly correct alto to any soprano air I might sing."

Amy certainly had early musical abilities, but the way she perceived and reacted to music was more unusual. When she was a toddler, Amy's moods could be manipulated by the music she heard. Minor keys brought such deep sadness that when Amy was being difficult her mother had an immediate remedy. She simply

By the time this photo was taken, ca. 1900, Amy Beach had established a reputation as a serious composer.

went to the piano and began playing the minor melodies of composer Louis Gottschalk's *Last Hope*. No more punishment was necessary. From earliest childhood, Amy also heard each key as a specific color. She would even ask for music by its color. "Play the red music," or the purple, or the pink. Throughout her life the colors never changed and remained vividly clear. Today medical researchers identify and study synesthesia (a simultaneous crossover of senses), but in the 1800s this was simply considered another peculiarity of the young prodigy.

Amy's mother had been a singer and pianist and was able to encourage her daughter's musical gifts. Like most middle-class homes of the era, the Cheney home contained a piano, and music was an integral part of family and social life. Before Amy could even reach the keys, she was drawn to the piano. By four she would pull a hassock up to the keyboard, clamber up, and stand to play. Within the year Amy was improvising duets with her aunt and playing the hymns she heard in church, complete with full harmony.

Years later, when asked how one learns to compose, Amy wrote, "Don't create music because someone says you ought to—write because you are impelled to write." Amy was impelled. The summer that she was four, she visited her grandfather in the country for almost six weeks. There was no piano within miles so Amy sought out the sounds in nature, listening to the birds as she walked and played in fields full of flowers. On returning home Amy told her mother that she had written three waltzes while at the farm. Amy's mother didn't believe it, knowing there had been no access to a piano on which Amy could experiment. But Amy explained that she had written them in her head. She went to the piano and immediately played the first, *Mamma's Waltz,* for her mother. Then came the *Snowflake Waltz,* and *Marlborough Waltz* (named for the street where they lived), each one complete and unique. Amy's mother transcribed note for note what Amy played, and the manuscript is still available in the archives of the University of Missouri–Kansas City Library.

By the time Amy was six, she could play by ear and sight-read printed music. Her mother began teaching her piano seriously three times a week. Two years later the Cheneys moved to Boston so Amy could expand her skills and have access to the best teachers. Her first memories of performing were private mini-concerts in Boston homes where she would routinely use her own waltzes for encores. As word of the prodigy spread, Amy's parents received many proposals for managing Amy, her tutelage, and her perform-ing career. They turned each one down, keeping Amy at home throughout her childhood. Amy's skills as a pianist grew steadily as she studied piano with several leading teachers over the next decade. Composing became a more frequent part of her musical expression, as well. At thirteen she visited with Henry Wadsworth Longfellow and, based on his poem, wrote "The Rainy Day". It became her first published song. The following year she took a single course in harmony, the only formal instruction in musical theory she would ever have.

Soon the time came for Amy to attempt the transition from local child phenomenon to serious touring performer. On October 24, 1883, Amy made her debut as a concert pianist at Boston's Music Hall. Billed third, Amy waited in the wings for singer Hope Glenn to finish. Finally, it was time. The slim sixteen-year-old walked onto the stage and took her seat at the Chickering grand piano as murmurs of curiosity about the rumored prodigy rippled through the audience. Long, brown curls fell to Amy's waist as she leaned into the first notes of Mescheles's *G minor Concerto*. She segued smoothly from the opening movement's power into the calmer, softer second movement, coaxing emotional life from each note. Then, with the control of a far more experienced performer, Amy's fingers moved up and down the keyboard, leading the orchestra into the fiery power of the final movement. When the last notes echoed through the hall, Amy stood and bowed, accepting the audience's applause. Even generally impassive orchestra members burst into applause, recognizing the young girl's virtuosity. Later in the program Amy reappeared on the stage, this time alone for Chopin's "Rondo" in E flat. The *Boston Transcript* later described her technique as "facile, even, and brilliant" and stated that "as fine as her technical qualifications are, it is the correctness and precocity of her music understanding that must, in the end, most excite admiration." Even the reserved *Boston Courier* announced, "Miss Cheney is evidently either a great talent, or a great genius; it is too early to declare which," while the *Boston Gazette* proclaimed the performance "the debut of a musical prodigy."

Amy was on her way and the musical world was expecting greatness.

Within a year she gave the first of many concerts with the Boston Symphony Orchestra performing Chopin's *F minor Concerto*. She began touring widely, giving an arduous twelve recitals between 1884 and 1885. Critics continued to praise her musicianship and superb technical skills in glowing reviews. But the strain of so much performing resulted in a sore finger by the summer of 1885. Mrs. Cheney took eighteen-year-old Amy to see a well-known Boston physician, Dr. Henry Harris Aubrey Beach. A recent widower, forty-five-year-old Dr. H.H.A. Beach was a consulting surgeon at Massachusetts General Hospital, a longtime supporter of the arts, and a pianist himself. Despite the age difference, the attraction was immediate and mutual. On December 2, 1885, they were married at Boston's Trinity Church.

Once married, Amy's life changed both personally and professionally. Gone were the loose curls or the familiar long braid of a young girl. From that day on Amy fastened her hair in a twist or bun. With her marriage, Amy was financially secure, and in today's world she would have been able to pursue her music full time. But this was a different era, and Amy was expected, both by her husband and the culture, to remove herself from professional performance and teaching and take her place at home and in society. Amy had already committed to a February 23 performance with the Boston Symphony, and reviews noted her name change, the end of her regular touring, and her beginnings as a philanthropist. "One regrets that so fine a musical endowment as hers should be withdrawn from a professional career" (*Boston Traveler*) and "The pianoforte part was played by Mrs. H.H.A. Beach [Miss Amy Marcy Cheney]. . . . She came out for an evening from the quiet of her home to gratify the public and to advantage a noble charity by the contribution to its treasury of the honorarium formally due her as soloist" (*Boston Journal*).

A year later Amy reappeared, playing a challenging recital of five piano sonatas to benefit the Ladies Aid Association of Boston's Children's Hospital. The *Evening Transcript* cheered, "Her exquisite technique seemed more finished than ever," while the *Boston Advertiser* noted her absence from performance commenting that ". . . it was with a selfish, but not at all unreasonable, regret, that the public [has seen] her sphere of action and her destiny change when marriage withdrew her into private life."

Although Amy's destiny had changed, her commitment to music had not. Amy focused her musical energy on composing. Dr. Beach was convinced that studying composition might interfere with Amy's natural style and originality, so Amy studied composition on her own by reading everything written about composition. To learn counterpoint Amy wrote out Bach fugues from memory and then compared her versions to Bach's scores. She used the same listen-write-and-compare system for studying orchestration. Soon her library of music scores and treatises was one of the largest private collections in the country.

Many music experts question whether her husband's influence limited Amy's musical growth, but Amy had a different view. In "Music After Marriage and Motherhood," written for the *Etude*, Amy hinted at one of the advantages she gained.

> . . . even for one born with the capacity for musical develop-
> ment, the greatest difficulty is to find the time for work. The
> constant interruptions that beset one who needs repose and
> time for reflection in such a career require much patience and
> considerable diplomacy to prevent their distracting influence
> from devitalizing and unnecessarily wearying the spirits that are
> so essential.

Dr. Beach did keep Amy from formal study, but he also gave her a lifestyle that freed her from routine household responsibilities and, by making her promise not to teach and limiting her performances, freed her to focus her time and musical energy on composing.

In 1889 Amy began composing her first significant work, a mass for voices, orchestra, and organ. Three years later her *Grand Mass, Op. 5*, was complete, and was premiered on February 7, 1892, by the oldest (and perhaps most conservative) music organization in the United States. It was the first time Boston's Handel and Haydn Society produced a work written by a woman. Rave reviews marked Amy's debut as a serious composer. Amy's *Gaelic Symphony* was next, performed by the Boston Symphony in 1896 and recognized as the first symphonic work composed by an American woman. Again her work was greeted with celebratory reviews.

Along with her major works, Amy continued to write individual vocal songs that became quite popular. "Ecstasy" was one of her most popular songs. The Beaches used the royalties from that single song to pay for an impressive summer home they had built on Cape Cod. Amy became a well-known member of the "Boston Group" of musicians of that period. Her music became known for complex transitions, flowing melodic lines, intricate harmony, and creative pedal work. Three major national and international expositions commissioned works by Amy, and she began to gain international respect.

Through all of this, Dr. Beach took great pride in Amy's growing accomplishments and, whenever possible, he enjoyed traveling with her each time a work debuted. When her *Festival Jubilate* was performed for the dedication of the Women's Building at Chicago's Columbian Exposition, he was by her side. He was thrilled to learn the King of Sweden had expressed interest in Amy's work when a concert at the Royal Palace included a group of her songs. As Amy gained increased recognition as a serious composer in the romantic style, Dr. Beach told "I am quite content to be a tail to her kite." But he was far more than a kite tail. Dr. Beach delighted in facilitating Amy's work as a composer, performer, and patron. The Beaches became well-known supporters of the arts. They opened their home for Wednesday night musical soirees that featured singers and all kinds of musicians, both famous and aspiring.

Then, in 1910, Amy suddenly lost the two people who had shaped her most, when both her mother and Dr. Beach died. Amy decided she needed a complete change, so on her forty-fourth birthday she embarked for Europe and the second half of her life. After several months of solitude, she returned to her roots as a pianist. Performing under the name Amy Beach, she began in Germany and toured Europe as a concert pianist from 1911 to 1914. Playing with many of Europe's finest orchestras, she became well-known and respected both for her interpretations of the piano classics and for her own music that she frequently included in the programs. But, with the beginning of World War I, Amy could no longer stay in Europe; it was time to go home.

Having rediscovered the joys of performing while in Europe, Amy wanted to continue touring. The challenge was balancing the time demands of performance tours and the solitude she needed for composing. Amy had always maintained contact with family and friends back in Henniker and Hillsboro, New Hampshire. Now in nearby Peterborough, an artist's colony had begun where writers, musicians, and artists could work in a wonderful blend of community and solitude. Beginning in 1921 Amy spent each summer in New Hampshire at the MacDowell Colony. She always stayed in the Watson Studio, and from then on most of her compositions were written there. The "colonists," as they called each other, were an ever-shifting group but, like Amy, many came back again and again. She became close friends with Colony founder and pianist Marian MacDowell, the wife of composer Edward MacDowell. She also enjoyed getting to know such diverse artists as Russian sculptor Bashka Paeff, playwright Thornton Wilder, and composer DuBose Heyward.

Amy had always enjoyed using the sounds of nature as inspiration for her compositions. When she was still a young girl, she had used her perfect pitch and keen ear to make a unique contribution to ornithological science. She worked with ornithologists, going into the fields and writing on paper individual bird songs as she heard them sung. Amy continued doing that throughout her life, compiling a collection of melodies that represented an array of native songbirds. At the Watson Studio Amy befriended a family of hermit thrushes. She transcribed their melodies onto paper and then incorporated them into her work. "Hermit Thrush at Eve" and "Hermit Thrush at Morning" became two of her most famous piano pieces. Each summer she would seek out the newest generation of hermit thrushes at the Watson Studio and listen to their songs.

For thirty years Amy spent summers composing in New Hampshire and winters doing concert tours. Despite her busy schedule of performing and composing, Amy always found time to encourage aspiring musicians. She would consult with singers in her New York apartment and sometimes would compose songs especially for them, occasionally even appearing in concert with them. Age was no requirement for her support. In the 1920s groups of piano students called "Beach Clubs" began to spring up around the United States. Often affiliated through the Federation of Music Clubs, the Beach Clubs paid tribute to Amy's beginnings as a pianist and celebrated the accomplishments of their role model.

A Beach Club in nearby Hillsboro, New Hampshire, was singled out in an article in *The Etude*. The accompanying photo showed Amy seated surrounded by three rows of young, admiring musicians bursting with pride and admiration. The writer challenged other musicians to follow Amy's lead. "If Mrs. H.H.A. Beach, the most distinguished woman in American music, and also one of the busiest, can take time to foster a musical club, should not others follow her example and fine initiative?" When traveling, Amy would drop in on a nearby Beach Club if possible, often giving an impromptu concert as part of her visit. She frequently visited the Hillsboro group and kept in touch with some of the young musicians for years afterward.

Perhaps Amy's desire to influence young students came from the encouragement of her parents. Perhaps it came from her own limited formal training. Despite her lack of formal musical education, in 1928 the University of New Hampshire gave Amy an honorary Master of Arts degree. The day was even more special for Amy because she was able to share the experience with her dear friend Marian MacDowell, who was given the same honorary degree at the same ceremony.

Four years later Amy was given an unusual coast-to-coast honor. The Federated Music Clubs that supported her Beach Clubs thanked her by sponsoring a program of Amy's music. For the occasion they arranged a complicated radio hookup and on March 15 radio stations scattered across the country simultaneously carried the program celebrating her work. Newspaper articles saluted both the music and the unique arrangement.

Amy also supported other organizations' efforts at music education. Active in the Music Teachers National Association (MTNA), Amy advocated a system of teaching pieces, graded by levels, for gradually teaching students specific techniques. She was generally positive but had strong opinions and was not above using sarcasm to emphasize a point. Having too often heard pianists attack the piano with unbridled ferocity, she submitted a proposal to the 1935 MTNA proceedings titled "A Plea for Mercy." She proposed playing pianos with tack hammers rather than fingers when playing in such a style. Clever and witty, her tongue-in-cheek article used humor to make people rethink some of the currently popular techniques without offense.

In autumn of 1936 Amy was suddenly taken ill and required hospitalization. Following surgery she was forbidden to perform any concerts for a year. As Amy struggled to regain her strength, she tried to finish some of the compositions she had begun that summer at the Colony. But she never fully regained her health and from then on wrote little and made very few concert appearances.

But Amy was far from forgotten. A group of her longtime friends and admirers began to plan a long-overdue salute. On May 8, 1940, more than two hundred composers, musicians, and friends came to a dinner in tribute to her, filling New York's Town Hall Club.

Eventually Amy was confined to her New York apartment, but she did not intend to let that stop her influence. Even without the strength to compose or perform, she could still write about music and she could still work to muster support for the musical causes she loved. The April 1941 issue of *The Musical Courier* carried a letter of appeal from Amy. The 1939 hurricane had done terrible damage to the MacDowell Colony and although Marian MacDowell had repaired many buildings, the Watson Studio chimney was still in need of repair. Amy described her memories of the hermit thrush who lived at the studio . . . "where I was trying to compose music, only to be constantly interrupted by his beautiful cascades of song" and asked that anyone who had enjoyed the musical results of her "efforts as private secretary to that bird-companion" send whatever sum of money they could so that the workshop will "again be able to welcome composers and birds alike."

For Amy's seventy-fifth birthday, concerts were organized across the country celebrating her music. The winter issue of *Keyboard* published her article, "How Music Is Made." In this piece Amy reflected on her life as a musician and the challenges that faced a composer. She advocated a distinction between types of compositions based on their purpose. She insisted that if one writes exercises, they should be called exercises, not portrayed as music. She viewed "music" as transcending mere technique and mechanism and achieving a quality of spirituality. America was deeply involved in World War II at that time, and Amy saw music as offering crucial gifts of spirit to a nation at war. She believed composers and performers not only had the power but the *responsibility* to use those gifts.

> Music must elevate. Because it is spiritual, it must give us courage
> to live and to fight for those things in life worth fighting for—
> whether we struggle on the battlefield or in our daily lives.

In late 1944 Amy became gravely ill, and on December 27 she died of heart disease in her hotel suite.

Even in death Amy continued to support the work of her beloved MacDowell Colony; she left all rights to her music to the Colony, which continues to receive support from her royalties. The appreciation was mutual. Ten years later, ninety-seven-year-old Marian MacDowell wrote a letter encouraging the Colony to finish raising a $10,000 fellowship "in honor of Mrs. Beach who was a fine composer and the first woman composer ever to get universal recognition."

Amy Cheney Beach composed 167 numbered compositions of chamber music, vocal solo and part-songs, graded piano pieces, church anthems, hymns, cantatas, and orchestral works. Her music is often described as overly sentimental or is downplayed as reflecting her lack of formal training. But Amy lived in a time when, as she described it, "Every middle class home had a piano, [and] young women were expected to learn to play and sing, and stay involved in amateur music making."

Amy, however, stepped far beyond amateur music making. She took on the role of society wife but used the financial freedom it provided to explore her music potential within that role and outside it. She became recognized first as part of the "Boston Group" of musicians and, eventually, throughout the world, opening the door for women to participate as full professionals in the composition of music.

Amy's debut was with the Boston Symphony Orchestra, and between 1885 and 1917 she appeared as soloist with them eleven times. Today the Boston Pops Orchestra performs at the famous Hatch Shell along the Charles River. The granite facade is engraved with the names of Bach, Handel, Debussy, Beethoven, and more than eighty other composers. On July 9, 2000, Boston Pops conductor Keith Lockhart led a program featuring the music of Amy Beach. The concert celebrated the addition of Amy Cheney Beach's name to that granite Hall of Fame—the only woman so honored.

HILDA BRUNGOT

1886–1982

Legendary Legislator

A MOVIE TICKET COST TWENTY-FOUR CENTS and a year at Harvard University cost four hundred dollars in 1930 when Hilda Brungot first campaigned to represent the people of Berlin in the state legislature. Berlin was then the largest city in northern New Hampshire, peopled by a large Scandinavian population but diverse with French and Irish sections as well. Nestled below Mount Washington, the highest mountain in the Northeast, Berlin boasts America's oldest ski club. Organized in 1872, the Nansen Ski Club reflects the city's Norwegian heritage. For decades, no one could join the Nansen Ski Club unless fluent in Norwegian.

Hilda Constance Fredericka Brungot was proud of her Norwegian heritage and belonged to the Scandinavian Fraternity of America. She lived "up the hill"—the area of Berlin known as Norwegian Village. Married at only eighteen, Hilda had six children before her husband left her to raise them alone. Working as a cook to support her family, she also rented out apartment space in her home. Always efficient and organized, Hilda soon had more

In the 1960s Hilda Brungot lost a reelection bid, took back her seat two years later, and graduated from high school.

apartments and took pride in being sure her tenants were happy. She and her family were well known "up the hill."

Norwegian Village was part of the Ward Three election district, and Hilda's father was active in politics there. Hilda had tested the waters of political service herself as a delegate to the state's 1930 Constitutional Convention, the first of five she would eventually attend. She discovered she loved having a say in the political process and at age forty-four decided to run for state representative. Hilda was a devoted Republican, and Ward Three was one of the few Republican areas of Berlin. But there were five candidates running and, as the newcomer, Hilda knew she must build a base quickly. Ward Three was the largest election district in the city, so legwork, publicity, and a personal touch were key to Hilda's plan. She enlisted the help of friends and neighbors, even her paper boy, young Donald Bisson, and his mother. Day after day for weeks, after he finished his newspaper route, Donald went up and down the streets of Ward Three hand-delivering Hilda's flyers at each house. Hilda spoke at clubs and neighborhood groups, took out ads in the *Berlin Reporter,* and talked to countless individuals. Just before the election she again sent Donald to deliver sample ballots house to house. An arrow indicated her name on the ballot. A "Thank you for your vote . . . Hilda" at the bottom added a gracious touch. If getting to the polls was a problem, Hilda had that covered, too. She developed a list of people who had expressed support but needed help getting to the polls. Working from the list, Donald Bisson's mother spent the day ferrying people to and from the voting sites in her car.

On election day all the personal touches paid off. One of three representatives elected, Hilda was at the top of the vote tally, winning her first of many elections and winning comfortably. In 1932 the results were the same, and in the 1934 election Hilda was so popular with her constituents that she ran on both the Republican and Democratic tickets. In 1936 she was again top vote-getter despite the overwhelming two-to-one Democratic presidential vote for Roosevelt over Landon. The following year the *New York Times* took notice of what was happening in the New Hampshire legislature. The headline read: "18 Woman Solons in New Hampshire: No other state legislature can count as many members of the homemaking sex." Commenting "some hide their ages," the article singled out Hilda Brungot, mother of six. The next year Hilda suffered a rare defeat at the polls. With six candidates running for three elected openings, Hilda received 674 votes, just 61 votes short of winning the third slot. Staying active within the Berlin community, Hilda was back in the winning column two years later and returned to the legislature.

Hilda was gaining quite a reputation in the legislature. She was an "active and aggressive" worker for the Republican Party. But she was even more an advocate for the North Country region of the state, fighting many vigorous battles to win support for that often overlooked part of New Hampshire. Her personality was always strong and she was not to be crossed. Tolerant of all races and religions, Hilda didn't stand for any black or anti-Semitic jokes being told in her presence. Known as a bit of a rabble-rouser, she believed in absolute separation of church and state. Politically, Hilda was respected on both sides of the aisle because she voted her conscience and her constituency and was willing to compromise only if it would help advance a cause she advocated. Some of her views were well ahead of her time, such as when she fought for labeling the contents of food products—in the 1940s. Also ahead of society were monthly "conscience raising" groups Hilda led at her home for women, counseling about the dangers of spousal abuse and encouraging self-sufficiency and self-confidence.

Hilda also showed concern for her colleagues in the House. Legislative sessions often extended well into the summer, and without air-conditioning, the State House was unbearably hot. Hilda often initiated a motion to allow men to take off the suit coats they were required to wear. (It is now required that a female legislator make the motion.) She also started a policy allowing smoking to start at noon when the House was in session. Hilda later stated that her motives were not simply a maternal concern for the men's comfort. Being practical, she knew that if they were more comfortable, they would be in a better mood, and if she had contributed to their comfort, they would be more likely to agree with her.

Hilda had strong opinions and felt obligated to persuade her colleagues of them. She required a cane and was known for using its hook to chastise an opposing representative. If she saw a colleague about to punch the red or green voting buttons in disagreement with her, Hilda was likely to thump them with her cane, resulting in a quick gavel bang by the Speaker. Democrats would avoid sharing the Berlin-to-Concord drive to the State House with her; they knew the commute would be a nonstop filibuster to influence their opinion on upcoming bills.

By nature Hilda loved to share her opinions, but as a representative she was responsible for knowing the opinions of her constituents. Politics, Hilda, and the telephone quickly formed a perfect storm over Berlin's Ward Three. Hilda spoke too fast, too loud, and too long. Donald Bisson recalled that Hilda called his mother almost daily, that Hilda "talked forever . . . you could never get rid of her because she ate and slept politics. She knew everybody and was always willing to argue politics." Longtime Berlin resident Donald Sloane remembered Hilda and his father debating politics on the phone for hours. Bernice Langlois noted, "Everyone loved to talk with Hilda . . . except when Hilda called in the middle of supper. She could talk and talk and talk, always with strong opinions, and you might as well forget your dinner!"

Hilda was a winning Republican from a 10-1 Democratic city. Her seniority was building, as was her political savvy. Hilda became known as a staunch advocate for often-overlooked northern New Hampshire. She was certainly insistent but also fair and respectful. All these traits earned power and influence for the homemaker from Berlin. When Hilda got up to speak, everyone listened.

Hilda was always willing to use any influence she had earned to help a constituent. Donald Sloane still tells his story. After World War II he had been on duty in Japan for twenty-five months when his father had a serious stroke back in Berlin. Donald was given emergency leave for a quick trip home to see his father. But Donald's mother had no way of supporting the family with her husband an invalid and requiring her constant care. She sent Donald up the hill to "Norwegian Village" to talk to Hilda. Having raised her family alone, Hilda understood how badly Donald was needed at home. Without hesitation she reached for her official state stationery and wrote a letter detailing why Donald should be given immediate compassionate reassignment. In short order he was restationed in Washington, D.C. But Washington was still too far from New Hampshire to be of help, so again Donald contacted Hilda. She had said that if her first letter didn't work, she would call her friend Styles Bridges. Bridges was one of New Hampshire's U.S. senators and headed the Armed Services Committee. Sure enough, one phone call was all it took. Within three weeks Donald was reassigned to Greenier Air Force Base in nearby Manchester, New Hampshire, and was able to take charge of the family.

Hilda took care of her constituents. She also stayed in close touch with her electorate, sending frequent reports on legislative activities to local papers and civic groups, giving updates in person to the American Legion, businessmen, or PTA, and connecting with individual people of Ward Three. But in the 1960s that suddenly was not enough. With the election of Kennedy in 1960, Hilda came in an unfamiliar third. Ward Three was down to only two representatives, and local papers announced, "The 14-term reign of Rep. Hilda Brungot came tumbling down Tuesday as Dems swept to victory." Even in defeat, Hilda was gracious. After each election victory she had placed a newspaper ad thanking voters. The day after her defeat she placed a boxed ad:

> I wish to express my sincere thanks and appreciation to my many friends who worked for me, these many years, while I had the pleasure of serving my ward and state as their Representative to the General Court. It has been a great privilege to have served you. [signed] Hilda C. F. Brungot.

Hilda regarded defeat as merely a temporary setback and was determined to stay connected with her colleagues in Concord. Still dedicated to the New Hampshire House, Hilda took a job as House telephone attaché during the 1961 and 1963 sessions and stayed in touch with both the legislature and her ward. Mounting a vigorous campaign in 1964, Hilda was one of two representatives elected from Ward Three and was just sixty votes shy of taking top billing once again. The traditional boxed thank you ad had a happier tone, pledging to demonstrate her appreciation and promising to "serve you at all times to the best of my ability."

Despite Hilda's pride in her legislative skills, she regretted that she had less education than most of her fellow legislators. Although ensured that all her children became well-educated, she herself had completed only common (elementary) school. In 1966, at the age of eighty, Hilda enrolled in night school in Berlin. She worked as hard in her high school classes as on bills she sponsored. As in the legislature, Hilda was not afraid to ask for help, often calling her son Clarence for help with particularly challenging algebra assignments. When Hilda finally earned her high school equivalency degree, she and her whole family celebrated.

Hilda's family again celebrated soon after when the New Hampshire Business and Professional Women's Clubs named Hilda "Outstanding Career Woman of 1968." Others were also recognizing and studying Hilda's lengthy career in the legislature. People began preparing for the fiftieth anniversary of women solons (legislators), including documentating their five decades since getting the vote in 1920. State House expert Leon Anderson began a book about New Hampshire's women representatives. As early as 1959 news articles had postulated that Hilda was the female state legislator with the longest service. In 1971 Hilda's standing as dean of women legislators in the United States was confirmed and trumpeted in state headlines. Special ceremonies at the state house April 8 commemorated the service of women legislators, with Hilda and others as guests of honor at the statehouse and governor's mansion. Leon Anderson's history was unveiled, and it asserted, "Mrs. Brungot has served in the New Hampshire Legislature longer than any woman known in any other legislative body in the *world*." He also crowned the city of Berlin as state champ, having elected eighteen different women, serving a total of ninety-eight terms in those fifty years.

Two years later Hilda was the sole guest of honor at a reception at the State House hosted by Governor and Mrs. Meldrim Thomson. Newspapers reported five hundred to six hundred people greeted Hilda with a "thunderous ovation" as she was given a pewter plate inscribed: "To Hilda Brungot, Dean of women Legislators, Lady of charm, with courage of granite. Presented by Meldrim Thomson, Jr. governor 6/29/1973." Assembled lawmakers from the House and Senate rose to speak in praise of their "Grand Old Lady." Family and friends listened as members of the Governor's Council honored Hilda's more than forty years of service, stating she was still as "peppery and argumentative" but "sharp and savvy" as ever at eighty-six. The *New York Times* reported on the reception affirming that when Hilda was sworn in for her nineteenth term the previous January it was "a feat said to be a record for a woman in any legislative body." Asked by a reporter if she was considering quitting or retiring, Hilda snapped back, "Not on your tintype! I refuse to quit. I'll run as long as God allows me and the people of Ward Three vote for me. I'll stop when my health gets in my way, not before."

Unfortunately, in less than a year, Hilda's health *did* begin to hamper her legislative work. After years of difficulty walking, Hilda had switched from her much-feared wooden cane to aluminum hook-on crutches, but her legs were still painful and increasingly unstable. During the following year's election Hilda was forced to campaign from a hospital bed, confined by severe phlebitis in her leg. Her newspaper ads pleaded: "Vote for Experienced, Friendly, Efficient, and Faithful Service . . . Hilda C. F. Brungot." But when the election was over The *Concord Monitor* opened its front-page results with the biggest news: "The longest political career in the state ended Tuesday when 87 year-old Republican Hilda F. Brungot lost her bid for a twentieth term in the state legislature."

This time, rather than staying on to work the phones, Hilda returned home to Berlin. The State House had changed. It didn't even *look* the same. Over Hilda's years of service the State House got new seats, new shades, a new rostrum in the Hall of Representatives, a new floor, and a new ceiling. When she began in the 1930s, legislators lightened the atmosphere with evening songfests and legislative bands. Impromptu mock sessions and night-long poker parties in the State House basement provided entertainment after adjournment. By the late 1970s hard times had necessitated budget controls, and the difficult choices added more stress. Issues had become increasingly complex, public scrutiny put legislators' work under a microscope, and individuals were often subject to loud public criticism. Hilda believed government had mushroomed and was now a business of its own. She very much regretted that somewhere along the way, the relaxed collegial friendliness was lost.

One of the collegial groups active during Hilda's tenure was "The Forty-Three Club," founded in 1943. In 1977 the group disbanded, donating its entire remaining treasury balance toward a permanent way of honoring Hilda. The Club, other legislators, and the New Hampshire Commission on the Arts organized a state-wide drive to raise an additional $2,300 for a portrait and frame for permanent display in Representatives Hall of the State House. The money was quickly raised, the portrait completed, and during a joint session of the Legislature, the display was unveiled on June 29, 1978. Hilda attended in her wheelchair and was celebrated with great fanfare, surrounded by family, friends, and former colleagues.

Hilda's mobility and health continued to decline, and soon she needed nursing assistance. Unwilling to leave the town where she had lived all her life, Hilda moved into Berlin's St. Vincent de Paul Home. When she died May 9, 1982, at age ninety-five, newspapers all around the state honored Hilda Brungot, "one of the constant forces in the New Hampshire legislature." Hilda had four sons, two daughters, twenty-one grandchildren, thirty-six great-grandchildren, a city of constituents, and a state filled with admiration for her lifetime of service.

The world of Berlin, New Hampshire, changed and struggled during Hilda Brungot's lifetime. In the decades after Hilda left the State House, the changes accelerated. Once a booming city of 22,000 with a thriving paper, pulp, and wood industry, Berlin's numerous active mills were closing one after another. Log drives became a page of past history. Today Berlin is down to 10,000 people, and not a single working mill remains. With no mill jobs left, Berlin is building new strength from old assets. Mount Washington now hosts a weather station cited in weather reports throughout New England. Fall bus tours bring "leaf peepers" out to enjoy the breathtaking foliage of the White Mountains—and to spend their dollars in local stores. Each winter visitors discover the beauty and thrill of skiing the mountains so familiar to Berlin's early residents. The ski clubs attract new winter sports enthusiasts. Resorts provide a seasonal boost to Berlin's population, and the Berlin economy celebrates the benefits of expanding recreational industries.

There are fewer legislators from Berlin today, but election campaigns are still hard-fought. Hilda's portrait still hangs in the State House, one of only three women so honored. Legislators know her name and occasionally pass on stories of Hilda's years of service, but with no one left who served with her, the stories are now second- and third-hand.

Donald Bisson long ago gave up his childhood paper route, but he did stay in politics. He graduated from campaigning for Hilda to campaigning for himself. Active in local and state politics for years, he has some of the same energy and know-how as his early mentor. Even in retirement his business card bears the familiar red Republican elephant, Donald's name, and a single caption: "Political Activist." Like so many other longtime Berlin residents, Bisson vividly remembers Hilda Brungot and speaks of her with open admiration. "You go through life and there are only a handful of people who *really* make an impression on you. Hilda was one of them. She was so smart, and so savvy, and so determined. Brilliant in her time. . . . Never could forget Hilda."

LOTTE JACOBI

1896-1990

Photographic Artist

DUST KICKED UP AS EACH YOUNG BOY scrambled to gain control of the ball in their noontime soccer pickup game in the town square of a remote Peruvian village. An old woman in an orange shirt quickly lifted the big Yashika camera dangling from her neck, twisting the knobs efficiently, and snapping shots. Later she coaxed shy waifs with large, solemn eyes from behind a door, disarming them with her smile. They posed for the American. Although she was with a group of tourists, University of New Hampshire alumnae visiting Peru, Lotte Jacobi stood out. Barely five feet tall and decades older than most of the group, her white hair escaping in wisps from a once-tidy knot, she seemed far more interested in the people than the place. Most of the group focused their cameras on the buildings, on the views, or posed in clusters beside photogenic town square fountains. Instead, Lotte photographed the local faces, catching personalities and shifting moods. Children at play, a woman and infant, a butcher at work, shy, yet curious children . . . each face told a story and Lotte wanted to capture each one. Portraying people on film was still joyful and irresistible for Lotte, even at eighty-one.

Lotte Jacobi with one of her cameras in her New York apartment in the mid-1950s shortly before Lotte moved to New Hampshire.

Lotte's fascination may have been her birthright. She was born in 1896 in Thorn, West Prussia (then Germany but now Poland) to the Jacobi family—professional photographers for three generations. As a young child, Lotte watched leading citizens pose for portraits in the family's studio, and by the time she was twelve, she desperately wanted her very own camera. Lotte's father wanted her to first understand the principles of light and lens and film. So he insisted she *make* her own camera. Giving as little guidance as possible, he watched as she labored night after night making her own pinhole camera. When the camera worked reasonably well, Lotte immediately began experimenting, photographing surrounding landscapes. By thirteen she owned a better camera and began photographing everything around her. She quickly proved worthy of more sophisticated cameras and moved on to complex subjects.

As a young woman Lotte married and had a son, but the marriage failed and in 1920 she moved to Berlin, Germany, to study at the University of Munich. Thinking three generations of photographers was enough, Lotte began by studying theater, acting, and filmmaking. For a time filmmaking held her interest, but she soon surrendered to the pull of photography and enrolled at the Bavarian State Academy of Photography. In 1927 Lotte joined the family studio, which had moved to Berlin. Perhaps due to her acting connections, Lotte's most famous subjects were leading members of the German theater community: Peter Lorre, Lotte Lenya, and Kurt Weill. She also photographed German intellectuals, including a young Albert Einstein, who was not yet world-famous.

As Adolf Hilter's power grew, Germany became a difficult place to live, particularly for those in the arts community, especially Jewish families such as Lotte's. When Lotte's father died in 1935, the family made plans to emigrate to America. Buying a round-trip ticket in hopes of returning home one day, Lotte was one of 1,085 passengers on the Cunard White Star Line's great ship *Georgic* leaving

Havre, France, on September 20 destined for Southhampton, New York. In New York City, Lotte quickly set up a studio and began building both a clientele and a reputation for outstanding portrait photography. Her first clients were mostly German ex-patriots who already knew of Lotte's skill. They in turn introduced her work to Americans they knew, and Lotte's clientele grew quickly.

For the next twenty years Lotte maintained an active studio in New York, specializing in portrait work. Lotte was known for capturing ordinary moments in the life of individuals rather than portraying her famous subjects the way she or the public imagined them. As in Berlin, creative artists were some of her favorite subjects. She photographed artist Marc Chagall, writer Maurice Sendak, actor-director Orson Welles, and many more. While moving around the creative set in New York she also met Erich Reiss, a concentration camp survivor, who had become a publisher. They married and lived very happily, with Reiss completely supporting his wife's professional work and delighting in her success.

Lotte's work was not traditional formal studio photography. She believed portraits should reveal the personality of the subject. Dispensing with the studio and placing subjects in their natural environment often relaxed them, allowing Lotte to weave her professional magic. Given the chance to again photograph a now-famous Albert Einstein, she scorned setting the genius before a blackboard full of formulas or scientific equipment. Instead Lotte went to his Long Island, New York, home and photographed a casual Albert Einstein first sailing and later pulling his sailboat onto the sand, trousers rolled up to his calves, feet wet and sand-splashed. She then photographed him as he sat relaxing in his worn leather jacket, hair rising in tangled chaos above his head. Oblivious to his hair, his surroundings, or the pen and paper filled with cryptic scratchings he held, a pensive Einstein seems intent on a distant idea, not a camera lens. The photograph created controversy, with complaints it was too ordinary for a man of such greatness. The now-famous photograph is typical Lotte work—offering a glimpse into the off-camera personality of the man rather than a stiff portrait of the icon. The two became life-long friends.

In a 1977 interview Lotte later described her technique for capturing the essence of a person's spirit rather than their image: "If I photograph someone I try to get them to talk about something that I know interests them, and then they forget the camera and I get their portrait." Asked how she knew when to snap the picture, she explained: "When I feel that the person has forgotten what's happening. I feel like a cat. I wait until the mouse is at the point." Lotte often used that skill to disarm even reluctant subjects, finding the perfect moment to pounce, capturing their spirit on film.

One of her most famous subjects, Eleanor Roosevelt, was notoriously reluctant to be photographed. Attending a reception for the First Lady, Lotte seized her moment in the receiving line to tell Roosevelt that she wanted to photograph her. After Roosevelt investigated Lotte's work, she cautiously agreed to a sitting. As usual Lotte made conversation from behind the camera. Mrs. Roosevelt was particularly interested in Lotte's experiences as a German refugee. As they talked and talked, Lotte's subject forgot about the camera. Lotte was patient, choosing moments Mrs. Roosevelt was the most natural and vibrant, to snap her shots unobtrusively. When the resulting photographs were developed and sent to the White House, one photograph so delighted Mrs. Roosevelt that it became the official White House portrait sent out with Christmas cards.

Not all of Lotte's work was portraits. Her husband became ill in 1946 and doctors recommended a diversion from his concerns. Lotte decided the two would take a class together from artist Leo Katz. Believing that the most important part of photography was not the camera but the light, Katz taught them to experiment with light, making prints and designs without a camera. Lotte found a way of moving light on paper to create abstract images she captured on photosensitive paper. Reiss was delighted with Lotte's new art of "photogenics." She also experimented with overlaying the photogenic's abstract images with traditional photographs. Best known are a series Lotte did combining dancers in motion over the swirling images of light. The movement of the dancer's skirt is mirrored by eddies of light and shadow, suspending her in frozen instants, mid-leap or spin, yet conveying energy, force, and power.

Exploring photogenics did help distract Lotte and Reiss from his illness, but the happiness did not last. Lotte's mother died in 1950, and Reiss died in 1951. Soon afterward Lotte learned their apartment building was to be torn down to make way for what would become the expanded addition to Rockefeller Center. It seemed time for a change.

Lotte packed up her belongings and left New York City. She moved to Deering, New Hampshire, where she lived with her son and daughter-in-law. John and his wife Beatrice Hunter had converted a summer home into a year-round guesthouse, and Lotte lived there for five years before buying her own cabin nearby. She continued to photograph leading literary giants, including poets Robert Frost, May Sarton, Marianna Moore, some in their homes, some in New Hampshire.

Once in New Hampshire, a whole new side of Lotte found freedom. On March 13, 1956, she entered in her journal "attended first town meeting." She was delighted in the open forum–style of New England town meetings and was soon a regular, quick to share her view on any and all issues. Townspeople may have resented Lotte's thickly-accented diatribes or rolled their eyes when she would stand up yet again, but in a town with two hundred registered Republicans and only five registered Democrats, Lotte apparently considered it her personal responsibility to sway the Republicans on issues. Over time townspeople came to appreciate both her participation and her ideas. Soon she proudly referred to herself as a "political animal" and for the rest of her life was active in local, regional, and national politics. After living through Hitler's rise, Lotte believed not "my country right or wrong," but "If it's wrong I have to do all I can to make it right."

In addition to politics, Lotte soon became active on local conservation committees and horticultural societies and embraced the natural foods movement. When Lotte bought a small hunter's cabin, it quickly became a palette for her newfound passions. In renovating the cabin she insisted on retaining its multiple levels so a bulldozer would not "carve up the land." The wood-beamed space added for her "studio" employed windows facing south and into a natural clearing. Wild mustard blossoms, white buckwheat, and a rainbow of wildflowers filled the meadow all summer.

Lotte planted herb and vegetable gardens around the edge of the clearing and nurtured a clump of raspberry bushes. Before long she added beehives, with 45,000 bees per hive. Lotte would pull on a pair of worn trousers and an old T-shirt and spend hours tending the neat rows on either side of her garden pathway, or with her walking stick bird watching in the meadow. Unexpected visitors might also find her, head completely covered in a white beekeepers' hat, white gloves to her elbows, standing on tiptoes to reach the bee boxes stacked four to five feet high. They often left with a jar of Lotte's preserved vegetables, jams, or honey.

Beehives were not the only stacks tiny Lotte struggled to reach. In a narrow storeroom off the workroom, stacks of photo boxes reached to the ceiling. Filing cabinets failed to contain the literally thousands of photos and negatives that overwhelmed the drawers and were filed in a folder system even Lotte often found incomprehensible. Every flat surface was covered in layers of scattered photos or projects. In other parts of the house were boxes overflowing with Lotte's latest auction finds, for she found it impossible not to bid on the most dubious orphaned treasures, needed or not.

Occasionally Lotte's pack-rat nature proved useful. For decades she had saved the return half of her Cunard Line trans-Atlantic ticket. When she began to consider a visit to Europe in the mid-1960s, she dug through the maze of treasures, portraits, and ephemera and came up with the unused ticket. Contacting a very surprised Cunard Line, she announced that she wished to use the ticket. Lotte worked her considerable powers of persuasion (and refusal to accept anything but what to her was only fair) and eventually the Cunard Line acquiesced. They honored the almost thirty-year-old ticket.

Lotte was a force to be reckoned with in any venue. In early 1960 she decided she would take courses at the University of New Hampshire (UNH). Intending to commute, Lotte announced at age sixty-four she wanted a driver's license. No one who knew Lotte was willing to undertake the challenge of teaching her to drive, so her family sent her to live at the YMCA in Manchester for a few weeks while she took lessons from AAA. Weeks later, a no-doubt shaken instructor informed Lotte's son that she needed a *lot* more supervised practice!

Somehow, on July 5, 1960, Lotte was issued a driver's license but was always considered a menace on the road by any who knew her. She became a familiar challenge to local police. Lotte often voiced exasperation that they seemed impossible to please. First they complained that she was creating a safety hazard driving too slowly down Main Street. Other times they stopped her for darting too quickly from lane to lane, or lane to parking spot. Her green Volkswagen was decorated with a hanging bell that jangled as she drove, a miniature American flag fastened to the windshield, and an assortment of decals and bumper stickers proclaiming her political platform. Between the car and her driving, Lotte was, as usual, impossible to ignore.

Transportation problem solved, Lotte did become a student at the UNH. She took classes in horticulture, art history, dry point etching, and even a class on the influence of contemporary television. She also took a class in French to prepare for her upcoming European tour. During her time at UNH, she forged deep friendships and a permanent bond with the university.

After her European trip, Lotte opened a gallery at her home to exhibit local artists who might otherwise be overlooked. Her exhibits included wood carvers, sculptors, potters, even a local violin maker. She would choose different artists and media each summer and welcome visitors, eager to promote the work of others at her gallery under the pines. The visitors flocked to see her gallery but also to receive guidance and advice. Lotte gave equal time to the famous and to young novices, poring over the visitor's work, reacting, asking questions, and discussing each photo.

Lotte viewed photography as an art form and fought for its recognition as an art rather than a mechanical process. She had been accepted into the New Hampshire Art Association in 1959, but as a printmaker, based on her early etchings, not as a photographer. She continued her work photographing an array of distinguished men and women. Pablo Casals, Marianna Moore, Margaret Mead, Benjamin Britten, J. D. Salinger, Thomas Mann, and many others found their way into her camera frame, each captured in a unique and revealing moment. Her subjects certainly recognized her work as an art form, and Lotte continued to advocate for her art and for the arts in general.

Lotte often said, "You can't live without art. Art is as very much a part of life as eating or breathing." Attending the 1968 Democratic state convention, Lotte proposed an arts platform plank. The times were turbulent and she argued that, "Art keeps us sane," especially in troubled times. After much persuasion, for the first time, the convention adopted an arts plank. Saying "no" to Lotte was an often-futile effort, as she took rejection as just a temporary setback.

In her seventies, Lotte's health declined and she was forced to close her gallery. She eventually went to Portland, Maine, for abdominal surgery by Dr. Ruby Day. Lotte had never eaten well and it took months of special care and diet for her to regain her health. Though Lotte was unable to work while ill, her career continued to thrive due to increasing interest in her art. Her very first one-woman show had been in 1959 at the Currier Gallery in Manchester, New Hampshire, a stunning exhibit of two hundred photographs chosen from almost ten thousand. Demand for exhibitions of her work had grown steadily in the decade since. While Lotte was recovering, numerous articles, interviews, and a hardcover printed collection of her work brought her a much wider audience. She had always been respected within the art world, but it was as if the rest of the world was discovering Lotte Jacobi at last.

Lotte became an often requested lecturer and keynote speaker. She protested that she didn't do lectures, but she would agree to "question and answer sessions." Her tiny frame almost hidden behind the projector, she would show a slide and then accept questions from the audience. Listeners often began timidly but were quickly drawn into lively and enlightening exchanges about the art and craft of photography. In December 1976 the National Endowment for the Arts awarded Lotte her first-ever grant. She was selected from 1,356 applicants as one of forty photographers to travel throughout the country photographing American photographers who interested her. Unfortunately a bout of pneumonia required her to stop the project before she finished.

Lotte may have been occasionally slowed by her age, but not for long. She spent countless hours during the 1970s writing editorials and protest letters, testifying on behalf of issues, signing petitions, any political action possible for a cause in which she believed. She kept copies of every letter, using recycled handbills, newsletters, and protest flyers for the carbons. Lotte was vehemently opposed to the Vietnam War and any use of atomic energy, regional or global, and adamantly supported conservation, limiting pesticides and chemicals. She gave speeches like "The Farmer Feeds Us All" and fought against razing local businesses for chain convenience stores. One letter urged newspaper readers to celebrate President Jimmy Carter's birthday and went on to itemize his assets and contributions, several years after he left office.

National Democratic politicians knew Lotte well. She had been a vocal delegate from New Hampshire to the national convention where Jimmy Carter was nominated. Four years later, when she mistakenly missed a deadline for her regular delegate status, she was crushed. Unwilling to miss the big event, Lotte used her still-formidable powers of persuasion and obtained a press pass to attend the event; she was the oldest press photographer there, but covered the convention gavel to gavel as it nominated Walter Mondale. She forged close friendships, both with President Carter and with the Mondales, exchanging letters, honey, visits, and photos with Joan Mondale for years.

As the 1970s wound down, Lotte was still going full tilt. In 1977 she went to Peru with the UNH Alumnae Association at the age of eighty-one and came back with treasured photographs of villages and marketplaces peopled by a kaleidoscope of children and vendors. She was also honored in the 1970s with a tribute exhibition at the International Center of Photography in New York City. The following year Addison House published a volume with reprints of both her portrait work and her photogenics titled simply *Lotte Jacobi*. The same year she received an Honorary Doctorate of Humane Letters from New England College, having already received one in Fine Arts from UNH, plus honorary doctorates from Rivier College and Colby-Sawyer College.

Around this time Lotte began to celebrate her August 17 birthday with annual blasts. From backyard picnics under a rented tent, to a supper and starlight boat tour of Lake Sunapee, to dinner at a Hillsboro restaurant, her friends eagerly looked forward to each year's invitation details. On her eightieth birthday she abandoned her usual T-shirts and smocks for a simple turquoise dress, but as usual skipped any cosmetics or other artifice. When presented with a red T-shirt emblazoned LOTTE FOR PRESIDENT, she immediately pulled it on over her dress and moved her ever-present Jimmy Carter pin from dress to shirt for the rest of the celebration.

In 1985 Lotte's ability to live alone became so compromised that she had to enter an assisted living center. At eighty-nine she was forgetful, didn't eat well, and often skipped meals for a day or more, but refused any kind of help. As always, Lotte made no secret of her opinions. She hated Havenwood and created a favorite chant: "Havenwood, Havenwood, Doesn't do me any good." Life became even more difficult when her son John died. Lotte was heartbroken to have outlived him. She attended his memorial service, but was obviously frail and often confused. She received many cards and notes from acquaintances, politicians, and colleagues. Still the pack rat, Lotte kept not only handwritten notes from Joan Mondale and the Carters but dozens of others signed with just first names of neighbors, students, and friends.

Lotte Jacobi died at Havenwood in 1990 at the age of ninety-three. In accordance with her wishes, there was no public funeral service, but newspapers, magazines, art world publications, and other media were filled with obituary tributes. Her ashes were buried beneath the crab apple tree behind her studio. Gradually the tree became a sort of memorial, decorated with film canisters, stained glass birds, and colorful trinkets, all of which would have delighted Lotte's sense of humor, practicality, and color. When the tree eventually toppled in a storm, it was allowed to rest and gradually be overtaken by lichen. With the colorful wildflowers, the lichen and mosses, and the dark bark, the tree calls out to photographers for a close-up to capture its personality just as Lotte had so often done herself.

Lotte bequeathed nearly 47,000 photographic negatives to the University of New Hampshire, along with boxes and boxes of correspondence and photographs. Her collection there fills seventy-two archival boxes. She is remembered vividly by many of her Deering neighbors, and any who knew her are quick to share stories of her opinions, driving, humor, and politics. But Lotte's most lasting legacy is the way she used her eyes and her cameras to chronicle the people who created the culture of her lifetime. When New England College bestowed a Doctor of Humane Letters on Lotte in 1978, the citation included:

> The significance of your art does not rest merely on the celebrity of these famous subjects. You have taught us that the eyes and the mind's eye behind the camera are as crucial as the subject before it. Despite your own technical contributions and mastery, you have proven that photography is not primarily technique but a humanistic and moral venture and that its obligation is to provide us with an authentic representation of the world.

Lotte was proud of those words about her art, but they address only one side of her. The Lotte that became a self-admitted "political animal" was committed to exploring issues, taking a position, and fighting for it—always working for her community, her state, and her country to be better. She often demurred when honored for her work. She was a truly noteworthy photographer, but she was also much more than her insightful photographs. Perhaps she would have most liked as her epitaph the opening sentence of the New England College's citation:

> Lotte Jacobi, born in Germany, citizen of New Hampshire and of the world.

BIBLIOGRAPHY

General Resources

Files, Collections, Exhibits and Papers

New Hampshire Division of Historical Resources
New Hampshire Historical Society, The Tuck Library, Concord
Milne Special Collections, University of New Hampshire, Durham

Periodicals

The Granite Monthly

Historical New Hampshire

LIFE

New Hampshire Profiles

Newsweek

Time

Local and Area Newspapers

Boston Globe

Concord Monitor

Manchester Union Leader

New York Times

Books and Collections

Batterson Jr., J. G. *New Hampshire Women: A Collection of Portraits & Biographical Sketches: Of Daughters & Residents of the Granite State, Who Are Worthy Representatives of their Sex in the Various Walks and Conditions of Life*. Concord: The New Hampshire Publishing Co., 1895.

Carnes, Mark C., and John A. Garrity, eds. *American National Biography*. New York: Oxford University Press, 1999.

Green, Carol Hurd, and Barbara Sicherman, eds. *Notable American Women: The Modern Period*. Cambridge, MA: Harvard University Press, 1980.

Johnson, Allen, and Dumas Malone, eds. *Dictionary of American Biography*. New York: Charles Scribner's Sons, 1931.

New Hampshire Notables: Brief Biographical Sketches of New Hampshire Men and Women, Native or Resident, Prominent in Public, Professional, Business, Educational, Fraternal or Benevolent Work. Concord, NH: The Concord Press, 1932.

New Hampshire Notables: Men and Women Who Have Helped Shape the Character of New Hampshire and Their Communities. Concord, NH: The Concord Press, 1955.

Tardiff, Olive. *They Paved the Way*. Exeter, NH: Women for Women Weekly Publishing, 1980.

Additional Specific Resources by Chapter

Eunice "Goody" Cole

Hall, David D. *Witch-Hunting in Seventeenth-Century New England*, 2nd ed. Boston: Northeastern University Press, 1999.

Hampton Library, Hampton, NH (unpublished notebooks, town records).

Lane Memorial Library, Hampton, NH (unpublished notebooks, town records).

Massachusetts Archives, Vol. 135 (summonses, indictments, court memoranda, depositions).

Tuck Museum, Hampton, NH (town records, news clippings, artifacts).

Ona Judge Staines

Archibald, Thomas H. "Washington's Runaway Slave," *Granite Freeman* (Concord, NH), May 22, 1845.

Chase, Rev. Benjamin. *The Liberator,* Letter to the Editor, January 1, 1847, as quoted in: Blassingame, John W., ed. *Slave Testimony: Two Centuries of Letters, Speeches, Interviews, and Autobiographies.* Baton Rouge: Louisiana State University Press, 1977.

Dishman, Robert. "Washington's Presidential Household: Family, Servants, and Slaves." Unpublished manuscript. Durham: University of New Hampshire.

Gerson, Evelyn. "A Thirst for Complete Freedom: Why Fugitive Slave Ona Judge Staines Never Returned to Her Master, President George Washington," graduate thesis, 2000.

———. "Ona Judge Staines: A Thirst for Complete Freedom & Her Escape from President Washington," 2000. seacoastnh.com.

Hughes, Paul C., and Paul F. Hughes. *A Pleasant Abiding Place: A History of Greenland, NH, 1635–2000.* Unpublished manuscript compiled 1996–2002.

Sarah Josepha Hale

Entrikin, Isabelle Webb. *Sarah Josepha Hale and Godey's Lady's Book.* Diss., University of Pennsylvania, 1946.

Finley, Ruth E. *The Lady of Godey's: Sarah Josepha Hale.* Philadelphia: Lippincott Press, 1931.

Fryatt, Norma R. *Sarah Josepha Hale: The Life and Times of a Nineteenth-Century Career Woman.* New York: Hawthorn Books, Inc. 1975.

Milne Special Collections, MC #61, University of New Hampshire, Durham, NH. Correspondence of Sarah Josepha Hale, 1830–1839.

Rogers, Sherbrooke. *Sarah Josepha Hale: A New England Pioneer, 1788-1879.* Grantham, NH: Tompson & Rutter, 1985.

Signorielli, Nancy, ed. *Women in Communication: A Biographical Sourcebook.* Westport, CT: Greenwood Press, 1996.

Harriet Livermore

Brekus, Catherine A. "Harriet Livermore, the Pilgrim Stranger," *Church History* 65, no. 3 (September 1996): 389–404.

Chase, C.C. *The Old Residents' Historical Association,* "Harriet Livermore." Lowell, MA: Morning Mail Print, 1888.

Davis, Rebecca I. *Gleanings from Merrimac Valley.* Portland, ME: Hoyt, Fogg, & Dunham, 1881.

"Harriet Livermore," *Southern Literary Messenger* 7 (February 1841).

Hoxie, Elizabeth F. "Harriet Livermore, Vixen and Devotee," *New England Quarterly* 18, no. 1 (March 1945): 39–50.

Livermore, Harriet. *A Narrative of Religious Esperience in Twelve Letters.* Concord, NH: 1886.

Livermore, Samuel Truesdale. *Harriet Livermore, the "Pilgrim Stranger."* Hartford, CT: 1884.

Newburyport Herald, January 19, 1827.

Harriet Patience Dame

Lake Winnepesaukee Historical Society.

Lawler, Lee Anne Rogers. *Dear Aunt Harriet: The Story of Harriet Patience Dame, Civil War Nurse.* Self-published, 1999.

New Hampshire State House historical resources.

New Hampshire Veterans Association historical resources, Weirs Beach, NH.

Senate Records from the 48th Congress, Report 762.

Mary Baker Eddy

Buckmaster, Henrietta. *Women Who Shaped History.* New York: Collier-MacMillan Co., 1966.

Dakin, Edwin Franden. *Mrs. Eddy: The Biography of a Virginal Mind.* New York: Charles Scribner's Sons, 1929.

Fettweis, Yvonne Cache, and Robert Townsend Warneck. *Mary Baker Eddy: Christian Healer.* Boston: Christian Science Publishing Society, 1998.

Koestler-Grack, Rachel A. *Mary Baker Eddy.* Philadelphia, New York: Chelsea House Publishers, 2004. From the Spiritual Leaders and Thinkers series.

Milne Special Collections, MC #152, University of New Hampshire, Durham. May Sarton correspondence regarding Mary Baker Eddy.

Powell, Lyman O. *Mary Baker Eddy: A Life-Size Portrait.* New York: The Macmillan Company, 1930.

———. *Mary Baker Eddy: A Life-Size Portrait.* Boston: Christian Science Publishing Society, 1950.

Smith, Louise A. *Mary Baker Eddy.* New York: Chelsea House Publishers, 1991.

Harriet E. Wilson

Gardner, Eric. "This Attempt of Their Sister: Harriet Wilson's OUR NIG from Printer to Readers," *New England Quarterly* 66 (June 1993): 226–46.

Gates, Henry Louis, Jr. "Harriet E. Adams Wilson," *Afro American Writers Before the Harlem Renaissance.* Detroit, MI: Gale Research Co., 1986.

Gewertz, Ken. "First African-America Woman Novelist Revisited: New Data About Harriet Wilson Revealed," *Harvard News Office,* Boston, March 24, 2005.

The Harriet Wilson Project, www.harrietwilsonproject.org.

White, Barbara A. "OUR NIG and the She-Devil: New Information about Harriet Wilson and the 'Bellmont' Family," *American Literature* 65 (March 1993): 19–52.

Wilson, Harriet E. *Our Nig, or Sketches from the Life of a Free Black, in a Two-Story White House, North, Showing That Slavery's Shadows Fall Even There By "Our Nig."* New York: Penguin Classics, 2005 (republication of 1859 original, with additional material).

Laura Bridgman

Dickens, Charles. *American Notes.* New York: Modern Library, 1996.

Freeberg, Ernest. *The Life and Education of Laura D. Bridgman: First Deaf and Blind Person to Learn Language.* Cambridge, MA: Harvard University Press, 2001.

Gitter, Elisabeth. *The Imprisoned Guest: Laura Bridgman, the Original Deaf-Blind Girl.* New York: Farrar, Straus and Giroux, 2001.

Hunter, Edith Fisher. *Child of the Silent Night: The Story of Laura Bridgman.* Boston: Houghton-Mifflin Company, 1963.

Lamson, Mary Swift. *The Life and Education of Laura Bridgman, the Deaf, Dumb, and Blind Girl.* Boston: 1879.

Laura Dewey Bridgman collection, Axe Library, Pittsburg State University, Pittsburg, KS.

Perkins Institute, Laura Dewey Bridgman biographies.

Sanford, E. C. *The Writings of Laura Bridgman,* reprinted from the *Overland Monthly.* San Francisco: Overland Monthly Publishing Company.

Simonds, Elsie Hurlbut. "Pencil-Writing: Talk Given to the Harvard Class at Perkins Institution May 12, 1951." Unpublished typescript in the collection of Samuel P. Hayes Research Library, Perkins School for the Blind.

Marilla M. Ricker

Barker, Shirley. "Marilla Was No Joke," *New Hampshire Profiles* 7 (September 1958): 20, 46.

Drachman, Virginia G. *Sisters in Law: Women Lawyers in Modern American History.* Cambridge, MA: Harvard University Press, 1998.

"Marilla M. Ricker, Washington, D.C." *The Law Student's Helper* 1 (1893): 304.

Richey, LeeAnn. *Reading Between the Lines: Marilla Ricker in the Struggle for Women's Rights.* Thesis, Stanford University.

Stevenson, Gertrude. "Sayings of Marilla Ricker, Who Would Be a Real Governor," *Boston Herald,* August 13, 1913: 2.

Marian MacDowell

Beatty, Jerome. "Pilot on the Glory Road," *Reader's Digest,* October 1937.

Brown, Rollo Walter. "Mrs. MacDowell and Her Colony," *Atlantic Monthly,* July 1949, 42–46.

Carmer, Carl. "Marian MacDowell: Woman with a Possible Dream," *Yankee Magazine,* April 1972.

Hillyer, Laurie. "And the Dream Goes on . . . " *Yankee Magazine,* April 1972.

MacDowell, Marian. "MacDowell's Peterborough Idea," *Musical Quarterly* 58 (January 1932): 33–38.

Milne Special Collections, Collection #15, Edward MacDowell, and Collection #154, Tonieri-MacDowell Colony, University of New Hampshire, Durham, NH.

Ranck, Edwin Carty. "The MacDowell Colony at Peterborough," *Musical Quarterly* 6 (January 1920): 24–28.

Wiseman, Carter, ed. *A Place for the Arts: The MacDowell Colony, 1907–2007.* Peterborough, NH: The MacDowell Colony, 2006.

Amy Cheney Beach

Block, Adrienne Fred. *Amy Beach: Passionate Victorian, The Life and Work of an American Composer, 1867–1944.* New York: Oxford University Press, 1998.

Milne Special Collections, Collection #51, 16 boxes, Amy Cheney Beach, University of New Hampshire (clippings, personal papers, journals, programs, photos).

Smith, Gail. *The Life and Music of Amy Beach: "The First Woman Composer of America."* Pacific, MO: Mel Bay Publications, 1992.

Hilda Brungot

Anderson, Leon. *To This Day.* Canaan, NH: Phoenix Publishing, 1981.

Also: *Berlin Reporter,* New Hampshire legislative records, election data, yearbooks of the Women's Club of Berlin, personal papers and records of family and friends, and personal interviews in Berlin and Concord.

Lotte Jacobi

Carlson, Martha. "Lotte Jacobi: Still Unpredictable at 89," *BusinessNH,* November 8, 1985, 77–81.

Dorfman, Elsa. "An Interview with Lotte Jacobi," *New Boston Review,* February 1977, 16–17, 25.

Goldberg, Vicki. "Lotte Jacobi: Sixty Years of Portraits," *American Photographer,* March 1979, 22–24, 31.

Hunter, Beatrice Trum. Typed personal memories and anecdotes by Lotte Jacobi's daughter-in-law.

Milne Special Collections, Collection #58, 72 boxes, Lotte Jacobi, University of New Hampshire (1898–2000: clippings, personal papers, correspondence, journals, exhibition programs, photos).

Samson, Gary. Lotte Jacobi documentary film. UNH Milne Collections.

Warnock, Phyllis K. "Home of the Month," *New Hampshire Profiles,* October 1963, 35–40.

Wise, Kelly, ed. Gentle Persuasions and a Benign Predator's Eye (Foreword). In *Lotte Jacobi.* Danbury, NH: Addison House, 1978.

ABOUT THE AUTHOR

Gail Underwood Parker has always loved New England, and since moving to Cape Elizabeth, Maine, she has often explored nearby New Hampshire. She is an educator, freelance writer, and author of published articles, columns, and books. She specializes in historical nonfiction and educational and parenting materials. A highly energetic and experienced workshop presenter, she enjoys inspiring teachers, students, and parents with down-to-earth techniques for improving home and classroom success.

Parker taught middle school in Cape Elizabeth, Maine, for thirty-two years, divided primarily between music, history, and language arts. Currently she is a parenting educator, with an emphasis on strategies for children who struggle. She is the proud parent of one adopted, four biological, and four long-term foster children. After writing *It Happened in Maine,* she created www .historyaliveinme.com, a searchable Maine history Web site. She is currently writing a book with A. Patricia Miller for parents of chronically dishonest children. Parker enjoys giving workshops anywhere and everywhere and hearing from readers, teachers, and students. She can be reached by e-mail at gailunderwoodparker@ maine.rr.com.